CHINA

The Grand Illusion
That Deceived The World

H. Richard Austin

Cover Image – *Over the years Shanghai's impressive, night skyline has captivated countless visitors, who fail to realize that ominous and terrible things are taking place behind so much splendor and brilliant lights. For a generation the well-orchestrated campaign of disinformation employed by the communist regime has been remarkably effective presenting a distorted image of that vast country. The popular belief is that through trade and commercial interaction, China is evolving toward democracy. In fact, the home of 20% of the human race is being transformed rapidly into an advanced, totalitarian state of chilling dimensions. Persecution and genocide are widespread and will only intensify. Also a massive, offensive military has been acquired that represents an imminent threat to the survival of the world's entire, democratic community.*

.

"The Art of War is of vital importance to the state. It is a matter of life and death, a road to either safety or ruin...the victorious strategist only seeks battle after the victory has been won... If you *know the enemy* and know yourself, you need not fear the result of a hundred battles...*Hold out baits to entice the enemy*... and [then] **crush him**. All warfare is based on *deception*..."

Sun Tzu, *The Art of War*

DECEIVE - to *mislead* by false appearance; to *trick* or manipulate others to their detriment; to *ensnare*. The "art" of subjugating others to one's will so they can be placed in a form of *slavery*.

This book is based on extensive research utilizing sources considered reliable; ongoing discussions and interviews; and the author's lengthy experience. Because of the difficulty of obtaining accurate information about a totalitarian state like China, what are considered reasonable interpretations and estimates are often used.

A companion work is available that examines the historical context in a fictional setting "The Coming of Armageddon - History's Longest Night" ISBN - 978-0-692-45238-7.

Readers are invited to visit the author's website - "TheComingofArmageddon.Com" where related information of importance is posted on a regular basis.

H. Richard Austin is a financial analyst who studies geopolitical events and their impact on the global economy and markets. His specialty is the arbitrage of currencies and precious metals.

TABLE OF CONTENTS

INTRODUCTION

BIG BROTHER IS HERE - NOW

THE GREAT CHINA SCAM

A POISONED REALM OF CORRUPTION AND BETRAYAL

and debt upon endless, meaningless debt. Pg.155

WORLD WAR III – PREPARATIONS AND STRATEGY

DESCENT INTO NIGHT

INTRODUCTION

In China the security police can locate and imprison anyone within an hour or two and often only minutes. Spy cameras (more than one billion) with advanced, facial recognition technology are everywhere in the cities (676) and even the countryside. <u>All</u> phone calls as well as communications on the internet and social media are monitored constantly. The movement of cars and trucks are tracked through implanted chips. 24 hours per day/7 days a week nothing happens in China that isn't observed by the government and a record usually made.   Over the years the vast storehouse of information that has been collected includes every aspect of the life of every Chinese citizen. The precise details of their face are known (46 criteria) and how those details have evolved. In addition to each person's location, it can usually be determined to a degree of certainty what they are probably doing. As a practical matter 20% of the human race (the current population of mainland China) is rapidly losing all freedom. In contrast to the laudatory reports that appear regularly in the western media, this is the reality of life in modern-day China, where the ultimate possibilities of tyranny <u>and the absolute control of human minds and bodies will soon be realized.</u>

Currently the number of prisoners in China's vast penal system (mostly slave labor camps) is so large it cannot be determined. This includes the widespread "black jails" and "re-education" facilities where people are trained how to "think correctly" according to the dictates of the country's new demi-god, Xi Jinping. In China, "Xi Jinping thought" is currently beyond dispute - *universal truth itself.* Throughout the country places of worship are being destroyed with pictures of Jesus Christ replaced by images of Xi, who has his own creation myth. Decades ago, a fatal number was tattooed on the bodies of the hapless victims of the Holocaust. Now every Chinese citizen is being assigned a personal number ("Social Credit Score") that is no less ominous - one that soon (year 2020) will dictate every aspect of their existence. For many the consequences will be no less ominous than if they passed though the iron gates of one of Hitler's extermination camps or Joseph Stalin's bleak Gulag of forgotten souls.

For years legions of pacifists and dissenters in China have been rounded up so their vital organs could be "harvested" for profit and the health needs of the ruling elite. This gruesome program has already claimed more lives than perished in the notorious ovens of Auschwitz. Instead of mass murder by lowly prison thugs, this most flagrant of collective crimes is perpetrated on a daily basis by highly trained surgeons in China's state of the art hospitals. It can be assumed that soon this well-organized program of mass murder will be expanded beyond the pacifist community to include anyone with a sufficiently low Social Credit Score. Similar to pacifists, such individuals will have fallen into that despised group regarded as "raw material" disposable to suit the needs of the communist state. Ultimately algorithms (mathematical formulas) will determine who in China lives or dies and whether they perish in a terrible way.

What is being fashioned in mainland China will soon eclipse what was imagined in the pioneering, fictional work about modern totalitarianism - George Orwell's "1984." In essence, mythical "Big Brother" has arrived in all his malevolent glory, and currently he is staring the global community right in the face. Already the puppet masters in Beijing are taking steps to apply the same level of control to the rest of humanity. This includes a massive, international data base containing detailed files on the people in many countries including most American citizens. The incessant hacking of domestic credit, medical and other record sources is not a random matter. This is especially true of those involving US government employees. Control by Chinese operatives of domestic retail, hotel and entertainment companies facilitates this insidious process.

Unfortunately the average person in the West is unaware of these developments while out of indifference or self-interest many in a position of influence knowingly disregard what such an ominous situation implies for the future. It might be questioned whether something so extreme really exists. Shouldn't there be more discussion about it in the mass media that focuses so much on political correctness to the exclusion of almost everything else? Why professionals trained to seek the truth could overlook something of such consequence is a story unto itself, and not an admirable one. Sometime in the future scholars will analyze the current era - that is, if they are allowed to do so. One of the central questions they will try to answer is why so many learned individuals could have acted with such indifference. In this regard grudging recognition must be given to the strategists of communist China for their skill manipulating the global community. In many ways they understand the present-day order of nations better than those who created it. This is especially true regarding the all-important role of trust built into the system and how easily it can be exploited and systematically betrayed.

Meanwhile a great, existential struggle intensifies on the world stage, the importance of which cannot be overstated. There are only two, possible outcomes - either the forces of democracy and freedom will prevail so humanity rises to even greater heights; or a dark age of oppression will descend like a giant shroud over the earth that can never be lifted. *At present this is a contest for survival that the world's democracies may not win.*

The nature of this rapidly escalating crisis is the subject

of this book. It is a crisis that showcases the dark, human trait known as "deceit" on a monumental scale. In fact, one can say with justification that what is involved here rises at times to the level of the unbelievable, especially the sinister intent. Once again the messianic role of megalomania has reared its ugly head, although who could have imagined that such a monstrous scheme could exist and it would be fashioned into something so malevolent. But the crisis is real alright, and soon it will impact the life of everyone on planet earth. From an historical perspective the situation involving communist China has its roots in the Bolshevik Revolution, when the modern totalitarian state was born out of the bitterness and chaos that Marxist ideology feeds on. That fateful event initiated a process that has dominated the last one-hundred years of world history. During this extended period various, authoritarian regimes have followed in the footsteps of the Bolsheviks repeatedly disrupting global peace. Although the 20th century featured unprecedented, human progress, there has never been an historical period with so much organized violence and widespread cruelty. Employing the most ruthless methods, the various, dictatorial regimes almost succeeded in their quest for unlimited power exercised by a select few. The margin of error between success and failure was very small. Meanwhile modern totalitarianism has not remained a static process but instead evolved with each succeeding regime profiting from the mistakes of its predecessors. Now in communist China this ominous spectacle is being refined to the ultimate degree behind a cleverly constructed façade that continues to dupe the global community. Despite the widely accepted claim the country is evolving toward democracy, China is rapidly transforming itself into the direct opposite. Advanced technology has facilitated the process, creating forms of human coercion and control unimagined only a short time ago. On mainland China meaningful dissent is no longer possible, and anyone who openly questions the government pays a heavy, often fatal price. Unfortunately many are still unwilling to accept such an unmistakable fact that is becoming increasingly obvious. The escalating conflict between the diametrically opposed systems of communist China and the democratic West will not be concluded peacefully. In recent years China's leaders have expended an unprecedented effort to assemble a massive, high-tech war machine. This ever-expanding, *offensive* capability can have no other objective except to achieve global supremacy through force - an aspiration rooted in Mao Zedong's fantasy of a worldwide, proletariat state led by the Han people. Since then this vision of a comprehensive, Marxist future has been brought into the 21th century by Mao's dedicated successors, including Deng Xiaoping, Jiang Zemin and now Xi Jinping. According to Xi's often cited statements that resonate with megalomania, it is China's historical role to reign supreme over other nations. The so-called communists believe without reservation in their grandiose scheme and are not about to change course. Those who control the most populous nation on earth have become the prisoners of their own perverse thinking and along with them the rest of humanity.

To a large extent the democracies of the West have themselves to blame for such a perilous situation. This includes the longstanding illusion that China's "red capitalist" economy will one day foster democracy. Instead a true viper was welcomed into the global family of nations and its economic system. As a result China has been able to exploit systematically institutions intended to foster openness and cooperation. *The Chinese economy has always been a clever deception controlled by the government - the objective to ensnare the unsuspecting foreigners and acquire by stealth and theft their wealth and advanced technology.* It is a regrettable fact that for decades corporate America and Wall Street have naively cultivated a working relationship with history's most lethal dictatorship and its focal point - the People's Liberation Army (PLA).

The communists have been extraordinarily successful

with their grand ruse and proven to be the superior strategists. While they understand the nature of the contest and act accordingly, the compliant foreigners have focused their attention on other considerations, principally short-term profits. To this day the situation continues to be misjudged with potentially fatal results.

In only a generation China has acquired the world's second largest economy along with an enormous military that continues to grow in size and sophistication. In many respects the capabilities of this military already exceed those of most of its democratic rivals. Fundamental to Mao's ambitions was always a great, armed conflict in the name of the people - the objective to claim a dominant portion of the world's resources and territory. Initially Buddhist Tibet and later the Muslim East Turkestan Republic (now Xinjiang province) were seized, in effect doubling China's territory. Recently dominance has been asserted over the vast South China Sea including its vital shipping lanes and resources - a bold encroachment already proceeding into the western Pacific. Meanwhile China is rapidly taking control of ports and bases staffed with disguised military personnel at strategic locations around the entire globe.

Soon to come the climatic phase of this epic quest for territory capable of accommodating China's enormous population. Because of the high-tech weaponry involved, the spectacles of World Wars I and II will pale in comparison. The assumption is that considerable time remains in order to prepare for a major, armed conflict with China. Unfortunately most strategists in the West have it wrong. As a result what looms not far ahead is not merely a period of great stress for the global community but rather a *precipice* that implies potentially an *abyss*.

And so the world moves inexorably toward a catastrophic war initiated by a dangerous enemy that for decades America has naively financed and abetted. In recent years a significant portion of the industrial base that enabled democracy to triumph during World War II was transferred abroad in the name of much-heralded globalization. Now this same industrial base will support the ultimate enemy of democratic values in what amounts to a life and death struggle for who controls the planet.

Because the rise of modern totalitarianism parallels closely the growth of democracy, it could be concluded that a historical chess match of grand portions is currently in progress. In the future will an all-knowing, authoritarian "state" built on Marxist ideology control humanity's destiny? Or, will it be a democratic system rooted in the Judeo-Christian, religious tradition and values extending back to Athenian democracy. This is the great, unanswered question of the current era with the most significant phase of this existential process approaching rapidly.

Not since the ruinous 14th century brought the Mongols and their cruel compatriot, the Black Plague, has there been a time fraught with so much peril. It appears that history is repeating itself with another great conflict emanating from the east. It is one that will showcase a force even more destructive than the worst biological plague - weapons that harness the limitless power at the heart of creation. In addition, this conflict of monumental proportions will illustrate to the ultimate degree what the ancient Greeks referred to as "hubris" or excessive, human ambition. This tragic flaw was the theme expressed vividly in the world's first great work of literature, Homer's *Iliad*. Not surprising, it was about a ruinous war that ultimately brought down an entire civilization.

The information in this book is based on research that has monitored global events for decades, especially in the Far East. If anything is incorrect, it is minor and does not affect the overall conclusions. What is documented here will not go away but only grow even more perilous. Now this rapidly approaching crisis is humanity's collective future that no one can avoid. To date, China's secretive regime has cleverly outsmarted the world's democracies like a giant parasite growing inexorably stronger on the lifeblood of its opponents. Is there a fatal flaw in the communists' grand strategy that once again will doom the dream of world supremacy inherited from Marx, Lenin and the violent Bolsheviks? Or have China's leaders engineered the perfect plan for seizing global power never to let go? Although at present this dominant question cannot be answered with certainty, it behooves everyone to consider the draconian possibilities that lie ahead.

Has a distracted West already lost this existential contest? Will a self-absorbed America weakened by petty, internal conflict and name-calling soon cross a fatal Rubicon and disappear into the mists of time never to be heard from again. Thus would end humanity's brief experiment with freedom and democracy that will have lasted only a few centuries out of the 3000-year span of recorded history - a noble but fleeting experiment that effectively doomed itself. At this point such a possibility is very real, perhaps inevitable. The debilitating, ongoing attacks on America and the belief in its unique identity should not be underestimated. In essence, *what is currently at stake for the global community is everything.*

"BIG BROTHER" IS HERE - NOW

1

Until recently no one imagined that something so insidious actually exists. Located in mountainous, central China, the vast assemblage of computers that is "Super Brain" covers several acres in a massive chamber carved out of bedrock. These are not ordinary computers but instead the type that process so much data they can analyze the complexities of a nuclear explosion and even the weather of the entire planet. At all times this huge chamber is eerily quiet except for the low-pitched hum emitted by so much electronic equipment pulsing with lights. It might be thought this ingenious device is actually alive and in many respects it is.

The limited human presence consists of a small number of neatly attired, maintenance personnel, who move about quietly like attentive drones. Their tasks are few because "Super Brain" is controlled by complex algorithms and functions almost completely on its own. It never rests and never will. In essence, this marvel of artificial intelligence is endowed with the ability to <u>monitor and control much of the society that created it</u>. Soon this will include whether most of those living in that society live or die and in particular whether they perish in a terrible way.

For any totalitarian regime to survive and prosper, one capability is indispensable above all others - knowing at all times where its citizens are located and what they are doing. This is especially true during a time of crisis. In this way everyone in that society can be compelled to obey the rigid dictates of the state and do what is expected of them. Previously there was no completely effective way to achieve this objective. Now that has changed.

On an ongoing basis Super Brain and the many facilities around the country that are connected to it monitor in real time ("watch") almost one and a half billion human beings. The detailed information that is acquired about every person in China is carefully organized and stored. Nothing viewed as important will ever be discarded. Of late, Super Brain's capabilities have expanded enormously so there is hardly anything it doesn't know about every person in China. This includes their *location*, personal and family connections, employment, income, spending habits, mode of dress, facial and physical features, the sound of their voice and even how they occupy most of their time. This data is regularly coordinated with all documentation such as driver's licenses, employment, arrest and medical records, etc.. In addition, personal communications through every, electronic medium are monitored constantly. Initially much of this data is kept at separate facilities for processing and then added to Super Brain, where it will remain forever.

As a result the government possesses an extraordinarily detailed picture of Chinese society and everyone in it - information that can be accessed in virtually an instant. The sophistication of the system is remarkable, and the possibilities for control truly limitless. The expenditure of resources and scientific talent to create something of such scope is extraordinary. No one should underestimate the insidious ways China's ruling elite intends to use this vast storehouse of information and is already doing so. *In essence, the Chinese people are the captives of this remarkable device as well as the dictatorial regime that is using it to assert an ever-increasing control over everyone in the country. At this point there is little that can be done to change this perverse situation that will only intensify and rapidly so.*

The data contained in Super Brain emanates from a wide variety of sources. One of the most important is the nationwide system of high-resolution cameras that include night vision and advanced, facial recognition technology. *These cameras are the system's* ubiquitous "eyes" *and are everywhere with the overall number already exceeding one billion.* (They are so sophisticated a detailed image can be captured over a distance of 100 yards.) Stationed strategically, they are in streets and buildings including business establishments, supermarkets, hotels, restaurants and bars, etc.. For instance, in Shenzhen City, where there is so much contact with foreigners, the coverage is 100%. This is also true of Beijing. The number of cameras in that sprawling metropolis is so large it cannot be estimated. According to official documents the overall system will soon "cover everything" (the actual terminology). Important in that regard is the use of "mini" cameras that can be installed in alleyways and tight locations. This is essential to the objective

17

that no activity, even minor in character, will escape detection.

There is also a program to provide blanket coverage of rural China - an enormous undertaking. In Sichuan Province more than 14,000 villages are already being "watched" on an ongoing basis. In Shandong 2,500 so-called "monitoring centers" are fully operational. An additional feature of the monitoring system in rural areas is that many images will be relayed to the television sets in homes and even to cell phones. In this way ordinary citizens will be enlisted to constantly "watch" their neighbors. This encourages the growth of a nationwide system of embedded snitches, who have nothing better to do except monitor those around them. Inspired by envy, revenge or some vengeful motive, they will be able to report on anyone, especially those they don't like. Now the disgruntled or unhappy of China will possess their own tiny portion of the government's malicious authority. Potentially everyone in a particular locale will be turned against each other so all sense of "community" is lost. What remains is only a desire to please the all-knowing state. Such an informant culture is essential to all totalitarian states. It has even spread to university campuses, where students are encouraged to disclose information about one another - the more personal the better. There is even a handy phone app that facilitates the reporting of rumors or casual comments at social events.

Recently the overall effectiveness of the system was enhanced when a mobile dimension was added. Police in the street now wear sunglasses that contain a tiny camera that captures nearby images including the faces of anyone passing nearby. If somebody has a discussion or dispute with a police officer, it is closely observed and recorded. Also at many, key locations cameras are present in the form of overhead drones that resemble doves with fluttering wings. Thus there is literally no place or activity in China that the eyes of Super Brain will not monitor.

If someone's image is detected in a particular location, especially a place of interest to the police, their image is identified almost immediately. *Within only <u>one second,</u> the system can scan <u>three billion</u> stored images employing 46 facial criteria. In what amounts to an instant, almost anyone can be identified.* In the future Super Brain's all-seeing eyes will only grow even more effective. This is the harsh reality of modern-day China - a captive nation heading toward absolute slavery that continues to be praised lavishly by the naïve and ill-formed in the West.

Because most moving vehicles are also monitored, hardly anyone can go anywhere without being observed. Tracking devices (RIFD chips with a distinctive radio frequency) are installed on windshields and the license plates of trucks, buses, taxis and private cars. This surveillance often includes cameras inside a vehicle and even an ability to listen to conversations. In the dual-plate taxis of semi-autonomous Hong Kong, such a program is widespread. Throughout the country conversations can be overheard at most locations where people gather for business or social reasons. This real-time, audible information is a valuable addition to the visual record. At the time of the Beijing Olympics, such a system was already in place. Lulled into a false sense of security by so much pomp and show, few visitors realized how closely they were being observed, including what they were saying about the regime as well as everything else.

While it takes only a few minutes to scan and analyze all of the personal information of any kind about *everyone* in China, the effectiveness of the system has been enhanced even further by dividing the country into grids assigned a numerical code. Each grid includes precise data about the buildings and households (including members) that are located within the assigned boundaries. Thus personal information is given a geographical context that includes any important events such as protests that have taken place within a particular grid.

Another category of vital data is being added that will expand the system's capabilities to the ultimate degree. This is a comprehensive DNA data bank that soon will encompass China's entire population. Containing each person's genetic code, it will enable the state to analyze their complete, physical nature including heritage, biological characteristics and even health defects.

Such detailed DNA data is significant for a variety of reasons. For instance, wherever a person goes, they leave behind a DNA footprint. If someone cannot be found immediately, it is possible to determine where they were until recently. This is especially important if an area is the site where something considered subversive occurred. Not surprising, the internal police are achieving greater success hunting down dissidents or undesirables. DNA data is being used widely in far-western Xinjiang province where at least two million Uyghur Muslims are currently held in large, concentration camps. In this way control of the entire population in China will soon extend to the *essence of each person's physical being and therefore their suitability to exist and for what reason.*

At all times the vast storehouse of personal data in Super Brain is accessible from police stations throughout the country. This includes the hand-held devices carried by most security personnel, who in public usually wear the sunglasses with a hidden camera. As a result every policeman possesses the ability immediately to obtain *detailed information about the prior existence of any person who happens to walk past.* A somewhat similar capability often extends to foreign businessmen, who live in China or visit on a regular basis. It is not generally known that most, hotel rooms contain hidden cameras so few guests realize how closely they are being observed. Unfortunately this includes couples in bed, who have no idea their performance is probably being recorded and will be reviewed at the local security office. For an evening they are unwitting stars in their own impromptu, porn flick. Perhaps the next time they visit China, an agent should be brought along so they are given reasonable compensation for their spirited efforts. In China, it is a basic truism that you are never alone - even briefly. Almost always there are anonymous eyes observing your activities, even those of a private nature. In a true totalitarian state such as modern-day China there can be no such thing as privacy, which is synonymous with not being controlled effectively.

In the last few years the sophistication of facial recognition technology has improved at an extraordinary pace. As noted, the face of every Chinese citizen is known to the smallest detail (46 criteria). Although the human face changes constantly, the problem of keeping track of these changes has been solved in a variety of inventive ways. Throughout the country faces are scanned regularly at places of business or when various activities are performed in public such as boarding a train or airplane. In China's schools and universities, a student's face is scanned whenever they enter a dorm or building and in the cafeteria when a meal is obtained. In class, cameras regularly monitor facial expressions to determine how each student reacts to the instruction being given. This includes whether they demonstrate the requisite degree of attention required by educational authorities.

Updating facial data has been simplified considerably by the development of the "smart phone." Almost overnight the combination of the smart phone and facial recognition technology has enabled China's nationwide surveillance system to take a quantum leap forward. Today such phones are an indispensable part of the life of every Chinese citizen. Without one, it is almost impossible to function effectively in society. Phone users constantly take pictures of themselves ("selfies") and exchange them with friends, who provide their own images. Also pictures are taken at social and business gatherings, providing a record of those in attendance and how they conduct themselves. Through various apps, all of this information is collected by the government. Thus the regime is able to acquire such invaluable data while expending little effort to do so. Instead the average citizen provides it on a voluntary basis. They even take a certain pleasure in doing so, believing that an enjoyable social game is involved. For the regime it is a game with a very serious purpose.

Another important use of the smart phone is the role it plays in the purchase of goods and services. Almost overnight China has become a "cashless society." As a result the smart phone is used not only for communications but also for most purchases. In addition, anyone who sells a product or service is provided with a symbol or code that is noted electronically. Thus a record is made of virtually every, commercial transaction that occurs in China - information that is promptly stored. Alibaba, China's counterpart to Amazon, is a particularly important component of the nationwide surveillance system. (Ironically Alibaba is funded to a significant extent by American investors, who are unaware that they have provided support for a key component of the world's most insidious spy system.) In these various ways the regime knows how the average citizen spends their money and how much they actually have. This information is enhanced by the fact bank records are monitored on a continuing basis. If any transaction appears suspicious, it is promptly investigated. Don't forget the government controls the financial system including all banks, depositories and insurers.

When interviewed, Chinese citizens speak with pride about the fact they live in a modern, "cashless" society. They emphasize that no other nation has moved so quickly in this regard. Of course, they are overlooking the fact this so-called progress has a sinister, underlying purpose. For many, this unfortunate fact will become obvious when they receive an unexpected visit from the internal police. Presumably a person only comes to their attention if something unlawful occurs. As a result most in China have learned to walk a very fine line, avoiding any act or gesture that can be interpreted in any way as objectionable. Of course, that is a matter of interpretation by those whose sole task is being suspicious of everything. For instance, all messages exchanged on WeChat, China's messaging service, are now recorded and stored permanently. This also includes *every action or inquiry* performed on the internet.

It is not enough for a repressive regime to collect

information about its citizens. Equally important is an effective means of preventing people's minds from supposedly being poisoned by information from the outside. Such unapproved information only encourages independent thought and hence subversive behavior. This has presented the Chinese regime with an intractable problem that it has struggled with for more than two decades. The result is the so-called "Golden Shield" that walls off the country's internet from the rest of the world. As a result China's internet operates largely in a vacuum in which the available information is limited to what serves the interests of the government. It is not surprising that Xi Jinping places so much emphasis on absolute control of the internet.

The most innocuous forms of behavior on social media can invite reprisal. This includes the use of many, apparently innocuous words or phrases. Of late, the regime has been adding rapidly to its list of allegedly subversive terms that everyone must avoid. This includes even a casual reference to "Winnie the Pooh" because many have noted a facial similarity between the childhood, fictional character and the country's exalted, new leader. With Chairman Xi being promoted as the country's most important, political figure since Mao Zedong, communist officials have not taken kindly to the comparison. In addition, the British, cartoon character, "Peppa Pig," has been banned because of the allegedly negative effect on young adults. Apparently communist authorities have convinced themselves that it is a subtle propaganda tool with negative consequences imported from the outside. These include the supposed glorification of lazy, overweight individuals who act in an amusing way while potentially undermining discipline in Chinese society.

The list of forbidden terminology goes far beyond fictional characters that appeal to the young. Not surprising, it also includes any reference to George Orwell's novels about modern totalitarianism - *Animal Farm* and *1984*. The long list of terms forbidden on China's version of Twitter include "personality cult," "*disagree*," "emigrate," "shameless," etc.. The list is constantly being updated. On Weibo, the banned terminology includes "Disney" (apparently because of a presumed connection to Winnie the Pooh), "my emperor," "personality cult," "incapable ruler," and once again "*disagree*," and "I *oppose*."

The use of the word "disagree" supposedly indicates a propensity for individual thinking that no loyal Chinese citizen should exhibit. These various exclusions demonstrate how arbitrary a dictatorial regime can be that perceives threats everywhere. Thus nothing is allowed that can be interpreted even vaguely as an attack on authority. For instance, China's National People's Congress has enacted a law that forbids any act or speech that can be viewed as a criticism or attack on the "deeds and spirit of the heroes and martyrs" of the Communist state - in other words anyone who at any time has served its interests in a noteworthy way. Thus an account of prior events involving such individuals can only elicit effusive praise because the people involved are permanently above criticism. This protection even extends to the family members of so-called "heroes," all of whom are entitled to retaliate promptly through the country's rigged, legal system.

With such a broad and ever-growing list of forbidden terminology, it is not surprising that large numbers of ordinary citizens are being rounded up and sent for a prolonged stay in the rapidly growing system of "re-education" camps. This is not a project planned for the future but one currently active across the county. The criteria to select the individuals targeted for reformation includes any act that can be considered a threat to "social order." Unwholesome tendencies can be demonstrated by nothing more than an objectionable image on one's smart phone such as rotund Peppa Pig. It isn't necessary to commit an actual crime but instead *merely demonstrate a "propensity."* Another consideration for being viewed as subversive is having a family member or acquaintance identified as a difficult person. According to a 2018 report on Radio Free Asia, nearly a million unfortunates are already being held in re-education camps so their "thought processes" can be corrected. This number will continue to increase as the relevant criteria are expanded rapidly.

Many individuals are held indefinitely because they continue to exhibit troublesome "characteristics." In such camps each person is subjected to a strict, daily regime that includes singing patriotic songs intended to awaken a deep fervor for the regime. In addition, they are instructed in various aspects of "Xi Jinping thought," the obligatory collection of aphorisms that supposedly define acceptable behavior. It is required that many of the songs and Xi truisms are memorized so in the future they can be recalled for immediate guidance.

As detention for re-education continues to spread, the authorities are emphasizing the draconian point that *how one thinks is a key component of acceptable behavior in the new China.* The parameters are defined in unmistakable terms such as absolute conformity to the party's stated policies with no deviation tolerated. This is a decisive change from the situation that prevailed for almost two decades when a certain flexibility in such matters was tolerated. Now there can be no mistake that is no longer true.

For instance, until recently there was a degree of freedom in China's universities. It was considered a harbinger of more progressive days that supposedly lay ahead. Once again another hope for the future has been shown to be false. Now it is clear that the strict dictates of party ideology must be followed everywhere, especially in academia. Even the slightest demonstration of independent thought is viewed as destructive to the national interests.

Not surprising, the pushback has been considerable. Many Chinese intellectuals view such supervision as a betrayal of long-held beliefs emanating from the tenure of Deng

Xiaoping. Nonetheless, party publications make clear that absolute adherence to doctrine as defined by Chairman Xi is obligatory. A new day has arrived, and there is no place for flexibility. In that regard meetings and seminars are conducted on campuses to make sure there is no mistake about the matter. If this "soft" approach doesn't work, it is obvious what the next step will be.

The inflexible nature of the situation is especially apparent regarding freedom of religion. Currently all religious belief is being replaced with an uncompromising atheism rooted in the Marxism inherited from the Bolsheviks. For several years a degree of religious freedom was tolerated. In fact, until recently such a right defined narrowly was recognized by the country's constitution. It is apparent this hollow promise was another elaborate subterfuge intended to mislead everyone regarding the regime's ultimate intentions. All across China churches are being bulldozed with sacred icons and symbols vandalized. A widespread tactic is defacing the image of Jesus Christ and replacing it with a portrait of Xi Jinping. Even churches "officially" sanctioned for decades have been destroyed.

It is now the stated policy in China that the party retains absolute control over all forms of religion such as Christianity, Islam and Buddhism. This also includes the country's traditional system of belief know as Taoism. As a result religious activities must always promote secular ideals -

what is referred to as the "sinicization" of religion. Those in a position of religious authority are being replaced by party officials, who employ what remains of the country's religious establishment to promote socialist ideals. The Central Institute of Socialism indoctrinates priests and others on an individual basis. Many are being forced into an extended residency in camps created for this purpose.

The treatment of Muslims has been particularly harsh with the incarceration of so many Uyghurs. In remote Xinjiang province information is difficult to acquire while Chinese officials characterize the camps as routine training centers. Unfortunately the methods employed go far beyond indoctrination. Hardly anyone has been able to leave these camps, and there are reports of some inhabitants being driven insane. What is involved is the potential extermination of large numbers. In that regard at least a million Han Chinese have recently moved to Xinjiang in order to inhabit homes belonging to Uyghurs. Obviously their prior owners won't be returning any time soon.

Religion of any kind is incompatible with the Marxist ideology revered by China's ruling elite. This is uncompromising atheism that views all religions as a force detrimental to state authority. A new day has arrived in China. The party is cracking down with increasing severity on all freedom of thought, especially anything that can be considered subversive in the vaguest way. It is apparent this draconian process will only intensify. *Any illusions about the true nature of China's advanced, socialist society must now be set aside. Dedication to the atheistic philosophy of Marx and Lenin permits no exceptions. During the Russian revolution the activities of the Bolsheviks illustrated vividly what lies ahead for the people of China. Soon Orwell's vision expressed in his novel "1984" will be vindicated and even surpassed.*

———————

As a result the global community will witness how far the communists are willing to go in their pursuit of absolute control while all individuality is eradicated in the ultimate, socialist society. Recently there was a major advance in this regard with the development of the so-called **"Social Credit Score."** This elaborate program aggregates and gives a focus to the various components of the internal security system. Specifically an arbitrary number is assigned to each person based on the various criteria considered significant by the government. Thus *a numerical "value" becomes a person's official* identity *that exceeds in relevance any other factor. In China's new-age, authoritarian society, it is the only one that will count.*

Although this numerical value vaguely resembles the credit score found in the West, it is far more complex and serves a very different purpose. Virtually all of the information that has been collected regarding a particular individual is analyzed to create this number. In addition to employment history, family and personal associations, the various factors include spending habits, the payment of bills and more vague considerations such as how that person uses their leisure time. For instance, someone who plays lots of video games on the internet receives a significant demerit. This is because such an activity supposedly indicates a shallow mind preoccupied with trivial matters. Around the country one can receive a demerit for merely j-walking - a revealing detail that indicates an individual who does not conform to established norms.

Those with a high score will be eligible for special treatment only granted by the state to those it favors. Thus everyone is encouraged to strive constantly to be acceptable to an exemplary degree - in other words a true, socialist being who at all times embodies Chairman Xi's exalted thinking. As a result the average person must constantly engage in rigorous self-examination and second-guess their every act. While living in a state of perpetual insecurity, each individual will nonetheless have the hope the regime will recognize their subservience and respond with appropriate generosity.

In China's advanced, totalitarian society no act is considered minor, and literally everything a person does will affect their Social Credit Score. The higher the score the better one's standard of living. Those with the highest scores get the best apartments, opportunities for high-paying employment, ability to borrow money, take vacations, buy a car and even travel on a plane or railroad. An individual, who has recently received a demerit of some kind, might arrive at an airport and discover that without warning their privilege to fly has been taken away. This prohibition would likely accompany the loss of the right to take a vacation. Typically such a decision is made automatically pursuant to some sort of formula. In early 2019 more than 17 million Chinese citizens were already prevented from buying a plane ticket, and at least six million a ticket for high-speed rail travel. Presumably this will prevent such individuals from spreading their unwholesome thinking to other locales.

Those with low scores will be penalized in every aspect of their existence, even the ability to have friends. It is important that high scorers avoid those with low scores, which will cause their own score to be lowered. That would be an unacceptable price to be paid, even if one likes that person and enjoys their company. In a true, totalitarian state there is no place for friendship or love. At all times the objective is pleasing the government and following its dictates so one has an acceptable life. Certainly no one would want to marry or date a low-scorer. Even in the sensitive area of human affection effective control by the government is exerted. Thus internet dating sites will be available only to individuals with high scores. Of course, those are the same people who have the best apartments, jobs and incomes. Under this system such factors far exceed the importance of whether another person might be viewed as a desirable partner. Few will like someone based merely on their looks, personality or kindness. This is especially true if an association with them requires living in a rundown flat with little money. Instead the valuable human traits of love and affection will be replaced by the need to conform and have a life with all the material advantages afforded by the state.

Ultimately anyone with a very low score will be marginalized completely and shunned as a pariah - in effect driven to the fringes of acceptable society and beyond. Merely being seen with such a person will entail an unacceptable cost. This applies even if the other person is a relative. Thus family structures will be minimized or eliminated entirely. Although based on personal information, one's Social Credit Score will be readily available so others know what it is. This is important, especially if a person's score has fallen so low that dire consequences can follow from merely being seen with them.

Before that fatal point is reached, a low-scoring individual can try to correct their "attitude" and hopefully over time improve their standing with the government. Such a change might take many years, but nonetheless the hope will still be there urging them onward to even greater heights of obsequious behavior. However, at a certain point reformation will no longer be possible. In this way everyone is trained to conduct themselves rigidly according to the required norms in order to avoid the fatal point of no return. Eventually it is inevitable that a totally compliant attitude will be pervasive in China and even passed down from parent to child. As a result it will rarely be necessary for the state to force the average citizen to act in an acceptable way. Out of the need to lead what amounts to a decent existence, they will do so voluntarily, at all times going out of their way to demonstrate compliance. No one will believe there is any other way to conduct their life. Already there are signs this slavish mentality is spreading throughout China, and no doubt it will eventually reach the extraordinary level of debased conduct witnessed in North Korea.

Supposedly the Social Credit system (allegedly formulated in 2014) is only being employed on a preliminary basis until 2020. At that time it will be implemented completely throughout the country. This time-frame is another convenient ruse. The average person in China might believe that for a while at least they still have time to let down their guard. Of course, that's the objective. There are numerous indications that the system is already fully operational and scores are being assigned to everyone. If the score is sufficiently low, it does not bode well for that person's future. For instance, the ban on plane and rail travel issued by the National Development and *Reform* Commission continues to widen. Also the growing use of re-education camps indicates the number being targeted for even minor infractions is increasing rapidly. The only hope for such unfortunates is to make a positive impression on their captors. For instance, this includes a determined effort to memorize the required, patriotic songs. It is not known who composes these shallow, repetitive tunes, although apparently it is someone with limited, artistic abilities who like so many are eager now to please the authorities.

A program already in use in some areas is the list of so-called "dishonest" people. Anyone identified in this fashion is penalized in a variety of ways that includes the inability to purchase a house or without warning having their assets frozen. Suddenly that person cannot function effectively in society. The criteria for inclusion on this draconian list is still unclear, although "threatening social stability" is a phrase often heard. This means, of course, questioning anything done by the government. Individuals in disfavor are even assigned a revealing ring tone for their smart phone that alerts all of those around them that someone is present who should be avoided.

Regarding the operational status of the Social Credit System, some point to the dozens of experimental programs that have been in use for years in various cities and provinces around the country. Some of these pilot projects date back almost two decades and employ a variety of rating criteria. For instance, in Suzhou the basis for punitive treatment includes such factors as cheating at video games. Thus if a person loses to someone during such a game, they can always retaliate by reporting them to the local security office. In any totalitarian system informants are always encouraged by the authorities even if they are only trying to get even with someone they don't like. (Many, hapless individuals ended up in Stalin's vast Gulag for the sole reason they were "denounced" by an unknown individual.)

In Xiamen, phone calls to an allegedly untrustworthy individual elicits the response by a computer-generated voice that a "dishonest" person is being contacted. Needless to say, not many complete the call or speak to that person again. How the suspect individual received such a designation is often a matter of guesswork and probably will never be known. Nonetheless, the sought-after objective of arousing insecurity and disharmony throughout the community is served quite nicely. In such an insidious context the only constant on which reliance can be placed is subservience to authority and the hope it will be recognized.

Over the years observers have viewed these various pilot programs as independent in nature and therefore difficult to coordinate. Hence it has been concluded that as yet it isn't possible to have a fully functional, national system employing the Social Credit Score. Actually all of these programs are merely variations of the same, longstanding project. In a controlled society like China no project of such importance would be allowed to operate independently or in a fragmented way. As noted, it is apparent that there is already a working national system based on all of this pre-testing extending back many years. This has been more than enough time to fashion a functioning, national system.

When the Social Credit system becomes "officially" operational in 2020, *it will be obvious that China's supposedly progressive "socialist" society has all along been nothing but a cruel, police state in disguise. This draconian, watershed event will rapidly transform Chinese society.* At that time the average citizen will discover that they have already been assigned the fatal "number" that is their official identity and henceforth will control their entire existence. This includes the ability to earn a living, enjoy the company of friends, find a mate or even survive.

The implementation of the social credit system on a nationwide basis is a key step in the regime's master plan for initiating World War III. It will be particularly important because of the degree of control it will provide. As a result anyone considered potentially subversive and uncooperative will have been identified so they can be dealt with appropriately. Suddenly throughout China there will be an accelerating incidence of late-night visits from security personnel. In situations considered particularly serious, the person involved might be sent immediately to one of the country's ubiquitous "black jails" that supposedly don't exist. This is because such facilities are moved frequently along with their unfortunate occupants. As a result when relatives try to locate a loved one, nothing can be found, even the jail itself. In China, all sorts of things constantly disappear, especially human beings. Those considered an even bigger problem will be sent to one of the many concentration camps in the remote hinterland far from the flashy cities of the Gold Coast - the ones featured so often on American TV. In that bleak realm a network of slave labor and death camps houses millions but like so many, ominous things in China supposedly don't exist.

Utilizing the latest developments in artificial intelligence, the nationwide system of data collection focused on Super Brain is already making many decisions on its own. This streamlines considerably the process of dealing with large numbers of people and placing them in the appropriate category so they can be dealt with effectively. Thus the regime can react proactively rather than waiting for a difficult situation to worsen or arise in the first place. When the available data identifies a troublesome individual, the problem of what to do about them can be solved in the most expeditious way. Why wait for something negative to occur that is already obvious. In China, there is no legal Due Process as the term is understood in the West. Instead there exists only a fake, judicial machinery designed to implement decisions made by higher-ups. Already an increasingly large number of the decisions regarding the average Chinese citizen utilize pre-tested "formulas." Eventually this will also include situations that involve life and death. Thus the problem of how to deal with truly difficult people will bypass needless encumbrances such as human emotion or ethical concerns. In other words *a person's* *"file" and hence their existence as a living being will be disposed of automatically when a <u>predetermined, numerical threshold has been reached.</u>* At that point intervention outside this streamlined process will be impossible and pointless.

Soon the level of internal control in China will far surpass what Hitler and Stalin were able to achieve. In comparison, their systems were quite primitive, relying mostly on informants and collaborators. The system in China will even exceed what George Orwell or Aldous Huxley imagined in their pioneering novels about imagined, dystopian societies of the future. When Orwell's "1984" appeared in the 1940s, many doubted that such an oppressive state could really exist. Now advanced science has made possible something even more insidious. As the slavish technocrats of China find new ways to imprison their fellow citizens, the subtleties of internal control will only increase. It is not an exaggeration that now the scope of what can be achieved in the name of unfettered tyranny is potentially limitless. In fact, the only limitation is the perversity of the warped minds that dominate such a system.

One of the objectives of any totalitarian system is to instill in its citizenry an abiding realization that resistance of any kind is futile. Don't question authority or take opposing action because it won't accomplish anything. You will only suffer the consequences, and they will be swift and unpleasant. Avoid the illusion of independent thought and aspiration. It is much better to be obedient and enjoy the benefits afforded the compliant citizen. Thus the human will is rendered impotent in the pervasive shadow of the all-knowing and all-powerful state. *Eventually individuality in China will disappear completely - a grim reality that is beginning to occur.* What will emerge is a prototype citizen who at all times is totally compliant. Already this has happened in North Korea, mirroring exactly what Orwell predicted after the ominous rise of the Soviet Union. It will have taken about three-quarters of a century and the rise of communist China for his predictions about such a dark future to be realized. The target date of "**1984**" isn't far from "**2020**" and the draconian events that thereafter will unfold rapidly.

The first, modern totalitarian state, that appeared in Russia during the early 20th century, followed closely the precepts of Marx's Communist Manifesto. Therein it is stated that communism abolishes all eternal truths including religion and all standards of morality. The substitute for such traditional guidelines is the all-powerful state that is always correct. Meanwhile the false claim is made that the interests of that amorphous entity known as the "common man" are supposedly enhanced. The price paid for this presumed progress is the transfer of power to a small cadre of all-knowing leaders chosen for such a role. In current-day China its ancient culture has for the most part been cast aside completely. As a substitute there is Mao Zedong's little "Red Book" currently updated by the sayings of "Xi Jinping thought" that is always available through a handy phone app. Of late, choice samples of such alleged wisdom are even recited aloud at weddings.

The emergence of a "shadow people" on mainland China is approaching rapidly, and soon the outside world will finally be compelled to abandon the foolish notion that commerce will one day bring democracy to China - the appealing illusion fed by the specter of unlimited, commercial profits. Ultimately those profits dangled successfully as bait before the international business community will disappear in a very harsh way. These same businessmen will be surprised to discover that the time has arrived when they are no longer welcomed in China - something that long ago they should have realized was coming.

Currently the regime's unprecedented, capacity for control is still being exerted in a subtle way so it does not appear overly intrusive. The screws are being tightened gradually as the system is fine-tuned and the citizenry trained in its inevitable role of total subservience. An informative example is the apparently trivial issue of jaywalking. In many cities across China, individuals who engage in this minor practice are being identified through their facial images captured by the ubiquitous camera system. As an admonition, pictures of the offenders are posted at crosswalks. Recently the ante was raised with such individuals receiving an e-mail that assesses a modest fine. The objective of the exercise is not to raise some money but instead inform everyone that at all times they are being watched and can be easily identified. From the regime's standpoint this is an important lesson to convey, and it is being done in an apparently innocuous way. The matter is anything but harmless and clearly points to what lies ahead.

As noted, an increasing number of people are already experiencing reduced freedoms such as those detained for reformation of their thought processes. In the name of combating alleged corruption, select members of the party no longer considered useful are being removed. Some have disappeared. No one is above scrutiny, even those who previously demonstrated complete loyalty. It is inevitable this process will intensify as the pervasive sense of paranoia that characterizes all totalitarian states continues to assert itself. The precedent for such a final, punitive stage can be observed in the Soviet Union, Nazi Germany, Pol Pot's Cambodia and elsewhere.

At one time the street demonstrations in mainland China numbered around 100,000 per year. Briefly they reached an estimated high around 180,000. Many involved 5000 participants or more. Typically they were unorganized and erupted spontaneously in response to some perceived injustice. Of late, such demonstrations are disappearing rapidly. This is a result of the county's enhanced surveillance system that enables local governments to respond quickly. In addition, police forces are larger and have more effective weapons to use against unarmed civilians.

A noteworthy development will soon make such demonstrations virtually impossible and simplify the task of suppressing opposition. This is a handheld AK-47 style "laser gun" developed at the Xian Institute of Optics and Fine Mechanics. Projecting a beam that cannot be seen, the gun is capable of igniting placards along with a person's clothing and even their hair. As a result they will be severely burned and potentially their flesh set on fire. If the beam impacts the face it will cause instant blindness. According to reliable reports, the gun will eventually be effective over a half-mile, the beam even passing through glass. Thus anyone who attempts to hide will experience great difficulty trying to escape reprisal. Because of this and other advanced tools of suppression, it will no longer be possible for any group to express opposition. Even the most determined will be deterred by the prospect of instant blindness or being burned severely by a beam that strikes like an invisible thunderbolt.

It is not surprising that large numbers of people are trying to leave China, although for most it is too late. Meanwhile in the West it is fashionable to learn Mandarin so one can move to the Far East and participate directly in the "great Chinese century." Similar to those who decades ago went to live in Stalinist Russia, such individuals eventually will be in for a very unpleasant surprise.

With the final stage of control in China approaching rapidly, the perverse reality of what lies ahead continues to be ignored by outsiders and even ridiculed by some as divisive propaganda. Also few appreciate what such developments imply for global society at large. When the final crack-down occurs in China, any belated recognition of the truth will be irrelevant. No doubt, the topic will become quite timely for informed discussion, especially on TV programs featuring "experts." Unfortunately such self-indulgent window-dressing will be a waste of time because the iron doors to the grand Orwellian jail that encompasses 20% of the human race will have already slammed shut with irresistible force. Then will unfold the final, inevitable act of this cruel and fateful drama.

Not surprising, top, communist officials are quite proud of how rapidly they are bringing to fruition the party's warped vision of a dystopian future. This is especially true of the increasingly large number of informers and snitches, who are being trained to oppress their fellow citizens including neighbors, friends and even family members. **The expression applied to this insidious activity is "*Sharp Eyes.*" This comes from the old Chinese saying - "The masses have sharp eyes." In that regard the descriptive word - "xueliang" is used that means "bright snow." In other words eyes that literally glow with intensity. Such a description is similar to what is often applied to fanatics and even the insane - the intense light emitted by the eyes of such people mirroring uncontrolled motivation. This revealing terminology provides an insight into how the regime in China views its** campaign of rigidly controlling the life of everyone in the country. As a result *no distinction is drawn between the obsessive behavior of those who facilitate this insidious process and what indicates madness itself.*

2

Bleak, disguised places dedicated to detention and death are everywhere in China. Most people ignore them while others try to convince themselves they don't exist. These countless, penal units of various sorts form what amounts to an enormous system of confinement and suffering that reaches into every corner of the nation. No locale is free of them because they are an indispensable component of China's new-age, socialist society. Otherwise it wouldn't survive for long.

In northeast China there is an ominous-looking, concrete building that covers several acres. It is surrounded by a high wall with a heavy, metal gate so it isn't possible to look inside and observe what is happening there. For years buses filled with people were seen entering the complex, although it appeared that no one ever left. After dark the building's chimney often emitted a nauseating odor that some compared to pigs being roasted. As a result there were lots of rumors. In China there are always rumors, especially about things connected to the government. As a result it's wise not to ask too many questions. Everyone knows of someone who didn't follow that unspoken rule. Often they disappeared.

This large, drab building with the heavy, metal gate was officially named "The National *Traditional Chinese Medicine* Thrombus Treatment Center." Its location is rural Sujiatun District south of Shenyang City, Liaoning Province. In spite of a name that evokes China's long and distinguished medical history, the so-called Thrombus Center wasn't a hospital. Instead for several years it functioned as a giant processing facility where large numbers of ordinary, Chinese citizens were systematically exterminated - the objective to "harvest" their valuable, internal organs. Gradually the most efficient methods of accomplishing this gruesome task were perfected. Now with subsequent enhancements, a sordid discipline of vast proportions has been developed that many in the Chinese medical establishment are quite proud of. The alleged crime of the victims is disagreeing in some way with the government or simply believing in pacifism.

Not far away is the huge Masanjia Labor Camp that provided any of the people murdered at Sujiatun. Upwards of 150,000 people are usually held against their will at Masanjia. Also in the area is the notorious Dabei Second Prison and the police office of the Huanggu District that specializes in advanced brainwashing. These types of facilities usually work together to implement the regime's program of intense social control and, if necessary, promptly eliminating anyone considered a threat to the regime.

As much as possible this vast penal system operates unobtrusively so the average person in China can avoid thinking about such an unpleasant subject. Also being imprisoned is generally regarded as someone else's problem and supposedly has nothing to do with a loyal citizen who obeys the rules. Of course, this means never acting against the government's interests or in any way questioning authority. Unfortunately that doesn't always guarantee someone's well-being. Suspicions can arise about things that are quite innocuous. Often no one knows why a person has been taken into custody and "goes away." Suddenly it just happens.

The so-called Thrombus Hospital was constructed in 1988 by convict laborers, who were removed immediately after the work was completed. As a result there is limited information about the facility, especially that it was specifically designed as an assembly line of death. The massive basements excavated deep in the ground can hold several thousand people at a time. Also in minutes the high-temperature crematorium can reduce a human corpse to a small pile of dust. In essence, the original purpose of this elaborate facility was efficient mass murder. Because human organs sustain life, no treasure on earth is more valuable. There is only one source - young and healthy human beings who are considered expendable.

After being extracted, the organs were dispatched to nearby hospitals where they were implanted mostly in people who paid handsomely for the service. Many were foreigners or so-called "organ tourists," who traveled a considerable distance for the service. Most went away quite pleased with the result, even if it is expensive. As a result organ-harvesting in China has become a highly profitable industry of vast scope. Also some of the organs are used to enhance the health of privileged members of the regime and the military. It is a valued perk derived from status. The substantial monetary proceeds go to the People's Liberation Army that from inception has managed the program regarded as one of the most successful in the entire country.

During the peak period at Sujiatun, upwards of 10,000 helpless victims were often packed close together in the dimly lit, poorly ventilated cellars. There was barely room to lie down. Only enough food was provided so the undernourished prisoners could survive long enough to be "harvested." Night and day the unworldly sounds of the extermination process echoed through the long, narrow corridors. Eventually the dreaded moment always arrived. Another hapless victim was strapped forcibly to a metal gurney and removed to one of the many, extraction rooms where the surgeons worked non-stop in shifts. There was never a let up, and at all times efficiency was emphasized.

After entering the facility, none of the prisoners would ever see daylight again, hear a bird sing or smell the fragrance of a beautiful flower. There was only the pervasive smell of unwashed, human bodies and unmitigated "fear." Uncertain whether it was night or day, the victims could only wait for the inevitable - their organs forcibly removed while *they were <u>fully conscious</u>. It is a key aspect of the harvesting program that only a tiny amount of local anesthetic is used. Otherwise the organ might supposedly be contaminated limiting* *its value - at least that's the theory. Also the "donor" must remain alive to the last moment so fresh blood continues to flow to all parts of the body. This means that the victim is compelled* to <u>witness their organs being extracted before their own eyes.</u>

Afterward what remained of a once-thoughtful human being ended up in the furnace room, where their remains were quickly incinerated. According to the limited information that is available, some survived the surgery and were still conscious when they arrived at the door to the furnace. The work there was performed by vagrants and impoverished farmers - their compensation the opportunity to scavenge jewelry or anything of value left on the bodies. Often this was a wedding ring that once espoused love. Now it was forcibly removed under circumstances involving the worst cruelty illuminated by the glow of a red-hot furnace. Sometimes there were gold teeth that were the biggest prize of all because of the quality of the metal. Eventually some members of the "hospital" staff were also disposed of in the furnace. This included surgeons who became uncooperative and ended up sharing the fate of their own victims.

It will never be known how many people reduced to the status of "raw material" were exterminated at Sujiatun. The information comprising each person's unique history promptly disappeared along with the vaporized corpse. In this way during the late 1990s there commenced in China a well-organized and highly profitable program of mass murder that continues to this day throughout the country. It is estimated that over the years at least one and a half-million people have been disposed of, or more than perished at the notorious Auschwitz death camp. In many respects this more advanced *"Holocaust"* surpasses what took place in the other killing sites of the modern era. Currently organs are transplanted at 700 state of the art hospitals that work closely with 370 penal camps. Many, top surgeons trained in the West willingly participate in the program. As a result what amounts to wholesale slaughter has taken on a certain respectability in the country's medical establishment. Foreign, drug firms profit handsomely from the medications that facilitate the process. Paying customers from around the world continue to flock to China's shores, their well-being enhanced by the vitality stolen forcibly from other humans. It is reliably estimated that the program produces at least one billion dollars of revenue annually for the continued modernization of the Peoples Liberation Army.

What is happening routinely in China is the ultimate version of the systematic "mass murder" that has played such a pivotal role in the international politics of the last one-hundred years. Initially the principal target of the program was the Falun Gong, a Buddhist-style, pacifist group. At one time its membership outnumbered the communist party - a situation the regime considered intolerable. As a result Falun Gong practitioners have been consigned regularly to various prison camps where they are always tortured. However, the principal strategy employed against them continues to be the forcible theft of their organs.

Nothing illustrates so vividly the mindset of China's governing regime and the cruelty that is commonplace behind the well-crafted image it presents to the rest of the world. In spite of the information that has emerged about Sujiatun and other extermination facilities, many in the West remain skeptical. Others prefer not to think that something so gruesome could be happening in a land with Confucius and Buddhist roots. This includes many businessmen from America and Europe who have forged profitable, long-term commercial ties with their counterparts in China and even the government itself.

As the evidence continues to accumulate, the nature of what is involved is undeniable. There are eyewitness accounts, tape recordings, detailed documentation, etc.. Essentially the record is beyond reasonable dispute. Hearings have taken place before the U.S. Congress. Various, international medical groups have repeatedly denounced the practice along with the European Parliament. Conspicuous outrage, along with the well-known slogan "Never Again," emanates from various humanitarian groups. Unfortunately none of this has changed anything. This highly profitable program continues unabated while occasionally the Chinese government issues another perfunctory denial. It can be concluded that soon *the program will be expanded to a significant degree, potentially dwarfing what has already occurred.*

From inception, organ harvesting was controlled by the notorious "610 Office" also known as the "Central Office for Guarding Against and Handling Heretical Religion Issues." (The actual name.) Presumably this title is intended to impart a modicum of respectability to the group, although like so many, phony names in China it is merely window dressing. The authority of the 610 Office comes from the Political and Legal Affairs Committee, an umbrella organization housing various components of the dreaded, internal security system. Because of the methods employed, the 610 Office is often compared to Stalin's KGB or Hitler's Gestapo. However, this high-ranking, extra-judicial group is even more powerful, its influence exceeding that of the police and even China's legal system. In essence, the 610 Office outranks everything except the highest segments of the government. Branches are located in every city and town, many state-owned enterprises (SOE's) and even some universities. Its representatives are literally everywhere and at all times have access to the nationwide system of data collection so people of interest can be located promptly. Because of its unrestricted mandate, the importance placed on the 610 Office and its harvesting program cannot be overstated. Instead its gruesome mission embodies what the Chinese regime considers central to its entire mission - the ability to eliminate promptly anyone considered a hindrance and do so in a way useful (and profitable) to the state.

The broadening scope of the 610 Office's responsibilities is demonstrated by the fact that recently it was formally merged with the Political and Legal Affairs Committee as well as the Ministry of Public Security. With communications enhanced, these key governmental bureaus can work together more effectively. As a result the organ harvesting is connected now directly to all security activities in China.

It is important to note the *inevitable relationship between organ harvesting and the new Social Credit System (SCS). In essence, the two programs effectively supplement each other.* Contrary to representations to the contrary, the SCS program has been active for some time with large numbers already penalized according to its amorphous criteria. The terminology applied to people with low social credit scores and those identified for harvesting is identical - "anti-social," "anti-party," "enemy of socialism," etc. The list goes on and on and can be applied to anyone.

After the Social Credit System becomes "officially" active throughout the country in 2020, those assigned a sufficiently low score will eventually be unable to function in society. Many will be driven to its boundaries and beyond. No one will be willing to associate with such people because of the risk involved. At that point these hapless individuals like those in the pacifist community will be fully expendable - in essence, viewed officially as "raw material" disposable in whatever way serves the interests of the state. Over almost a quarter century, a vast and efficient apparatus has been created in China that is dedicated to this gruesome premise. It is only reasonable to conclude that the regime will continue to expand a program that has served its needs so effectively. The Social Credit Score provides the perfect means to do so.

The difficulty of locating individuals with useful organs is lessened considerably because so much information is now available about everyone in the country. This includes their detailed health data. While exchanging "selfies" on their up-to-date smart phones and expressing themselves openly on social media, most people fail to appreciate the reality of what awaits them in the not-distant future. When the Social Credit program becomes officially active, the full implications of what is involved will soon become apparent. Those, who haven't demonstrated the requisite degree of subservience, will discover that they have already been assigned a score sufficiently low to qualify them for organ harvesting or something even worse.

At any time a low scorer can expect a late-night knock on the door, and when it is opened, there will stand the blank-faced members of a well-armed, harvesting squad. In hand will be a computer-generated form printed automatically pursuant to the applicable algorithm. For years, legions of ordinary Chinese citizens have been carted away for disposal and all trace of their existence obliterated - a dreaded spectacle generally regarded as someone else's problem. That will no longer be the case. The demand for useful organs continues to expand as inventive ways are found for them in China's huge, medical system. This is especially true of those facilities serving the health needs of the regime. In time of war the need for fresh organs will increase rapidly. With the advent of the Social Credit system the program will never run out of useful bodies.

Essentially the systematic murder of pacifists such as the Falun Gong was merely a warm-up for what is to come. With the number of useful organs currently limited, it is inevitable that the harvesting program will be expanded to other segments of the population. This includes the occupants of select, geographical areas. In the detention camps of Xinjiang Province, the blood tests that precede the theft of one's organs are supposedly being administered. These tests are expensive and only done with one purpose in mind. It is likely that other locales are also involved, including Tibet that continues to resist the destruction of its culture. In this way one of communist China's most effective and profitable programs will continue to grow and flourish.

Beginning sometime in 2020 the fate of 20% of the human race will be determined by a numerical designation synthesized by a computer. For some individuals this will result in the harshest fate. Because not everyone with a low credit score will be eligible for harvesting, the question arises about what should be done with such "undesirables." In China there continues to be extensive research into various forms of "mind control" with considerable progress already achieved. Research into human cognition is conducted in many top universities such as Ningbo University, Beijing Normal University and others. Often this research is closely coordinated with real-life situations such as manufacturing plants. For instance, many assembly line employees are required to wear special hats that enable their brainwaves to be monitored and recorded on a real-time basis. As a result their emotions and brainwaves can be analyzed while they perform various tasks, especially those of a repetitive nature. In addition, this information is coordinated with the person's facial expressions. In this way it is possible to know exactly how the employee reacts to stimuli and whether they are functioning in the most productive way.

It is claimed this brain-monitoring program is nothing more than a benign effort to improve safety and performance in the workplace. Like everything in China there is always the innocuous explanation that obscures the harsh truth about what is really involved. The ultimate goal is nothing less than the ability to "manipulate" human thought itself - the holy grail of all totalitarian states. Till now that wasn't possible because the requisite technology was lacking. Eventually the experimental hat worn by the subjects in these studies can be replaced by an electronic chip inserted under the scalp or even into the brain itself. Essentially a microprocessor, it would become a part of the brain's circuitry that is electrical in nature. Thus a person's behavior can be programmed beforehand or even controlled from a remote location. In essence, those with sufficiently low credit scores, who are not eligible for the harvesting program, will be turned into automatons or a form of human robot. From the regime's perspective this would be far more advantageous than expending resources to imprison or execute such undesirables. Furthermore it would provide the means to have many, unappealing tasks considered important to society performed in an efficient manner. In this way the individual involved would be incapable of not following the required procedures and meeting deadlines. Already such an electronic chip is under development.

While this gruesome prospect might seem far-fetched, the topic should be viewed in the context of the methods employed in the organ harvesting program, especially the limited use of anesthetics. For years an extensive effort to control human thought has been conducted in China's psychiatric hospitals employing mind-altering chemicals - a program that has its roots in the Soviet Union. When all else fails, these facilities can always be counted on to induce the requisite subservience. It is not possible to know the exact number of "patients" in these facilities, although it is considerable. Not surprising, such locations are referred to with another of those misleading ("doublespeak") names that proliferate in China - "Ankang," which means *"peace and health*" with emphasis on the first term. Presumably the sense of peace referred to is the oblivion experienced by the anesthetized individual whose mind is slowly being erased. For years chemical regimens have been employed with considerable success to pacify dissidents, especially civil rights lawyers. After an extensive application of such substances, it is not surprising that many of these individuals can no longer think effectively. Like other enhancements in technology, the regime in China has not overlooked the possibilities of control afforded by the hypodermic needle.

Because of the varied effects of such chemicals, the results continue to be inexact. Often the person involved is incapable of performing any useful task. Thus while no longer a threat to the government, the individual pacified by chemical means is reduced to what amounts to a useless zombie that ultimately must be disposed of. In contrast, pre-programmed, electronic devices connected to the brain overcome such problems. Manipulating the minds of supposedly undesirable people in the service of the state is a logical next step for a country moving rapidly toward the final frontiers of absolute tyranny. Considering the rapid growth of the applicable technology, this additional development is not far away. For those with a sufficiently low social credit score, organ harvesting might be the preferable alternative because at least there would be an end to the torment. And finally it should be noted that evidence has emerged that China's scientists are conducting extensive experiments altering the brains of animals such as monkeys with implants. Also the brains of unborn humans are being manipulated through bio-engineering technology (CRISPN). One of the objectives is eventually to create super-intelligent individuals - in essence, a new super-race. How often have other discredited regimes pursued a similar aspiration.

Meanwhile the global, community continues to disregard the fact a society potentially more sinister than what is portrayed in Orwell's "1984" is developing rapidly on the Chinese mainland. At the same time this society continues to be praised effusively for its economic progress. Many Americans have invested their life savings, including retirement funds, in various aspects of the so-called China "miracle." What they are really investing in is a political entity that embodies everything appalling that visionaries have long predicted about a dystopian future dominated by the schemes of the far left (Marxism).

When a human being is reduced by a government to the status of useful "raw material," there is no limit to what is possible and inevitable. At this point the appalling fact of what the Chinese communist state is really about is becoming increasingly obvious. Presumably at some point America's mass media will finally awaken to the reality of where the real threat to human liberty resides. **Based on the gruesome record of war and genocide during the last century, it cannot be** said that once again humanity hasn't been given a fair warning. This time the surprise will be how far communist China's governing regime is willing to go in order to implement its grandiose schemes. At this point it possesses sufficient, advanced technology and a critical mass of people to do virtually anything it wants.

3

While China's repressive government rapidly asserts control over the huge population of the mainland, its far-reaching tentacles extend outward into every corner of the world. The regime's quest for power has gone global with subversion masquerading as economic cooperation on a grand scale. The objective is nothing less than controlling global society itself. To a significant extent through stealth this far-reaching capability is being acquired rapidly.

The much-heralded project known as "One Belt/ One Road" (OBOR) supposedly harkens back to the medieval, trade route between Asia and Europe. As a result this recent, more ambitious version is often referred to as the "New Silk Road." The stated objective is the creation of a vast network of roads, rail lines and ports that binds together the Asian continent with Europe, the Middle East and Africa. Potentially more than 100 countries will be involved representing at least two-thirds of the world's population. The cost has been variously estimated at upwards of four trillion $US. It is an unprecedented undertaking of remarkable scope.

In this way a major portion of the world will be connected by land and sea directly to China's manufacturing base. Raw materials will flow into China, and the finished goods in the opposite direction. There are two, main components: land and rail corridors principally in Asia and

Europe; and secondly, maritime passageways that literally span the globe. This includes strategic locations at or near key "chokepoints" that dominate international transport. Of late, *it is becoming increasingly apparent that the real significance of the OBOR project is not economic but instead military.*

Despite the overwhelming benefits that accrue to China, almost the entire cost of the project will be subsidized by the participating countries. Literally they pay for the privilege of furthering Chinese interests. At select locations around the world, elaborate transport and port facilities are being constructed using high-interest credits from China's government-owned banks. In fact, many of the nations involved lack the ability to support the liability being incurred. China's operatives are well-aware of this fact, and that's the point. Along the way lots of misleading salesmanship is employed that emphasizes the importance of belonging to such a far-reaching scheme. In this way vulnerable, Third World countries continue to be lured into escalating financial arrangements that will lead inevitably to default. For some this has already happened. In this way China takes control of the project along with the territory on which it is built and sometimes other assets as well. In addition, the all-important sovereignty of the country involved is seriously compromised.

The consequences of the self-serving OBOR project should be viewed in the context of China's long-standing appetite for strategic territory belonging to others. In essence, this process of global encroachment is nothing new - only the method that is employed. Decades ago China unilaterally seized the independent, Buddhist nation of Tibet with large portions of its territory incorporated immediately into Sichuan, Qinghai, Gansu and Yunnan Provinces. A key objective of this bold act is control of the valuable water resources of the Tibetan highlands - the source of seven of the world's major rivers including the Brahmaputra in India and the Mekong in Southeast Asia. It is no secret that eventually China intends to expropriate large portions of this water to replenish its own resources badly depleted by years of overly rapid industrialization.

Following the acquisition of Tibet, the Muslim East Turkestan Republic (now Xinjiang Province) was also seized. These two, forced acquisitions increased China's overall size by nearly one-half of what exists today. In addition to important natural resources, the territory acquired improved significantly China's overall, strategic position, especially in relationship to traditional enemies.

Since once-independent Tibet and East Turkestan were acquired, there has been an ongoing effort to extinguish the indigenous cultures along with the established identity of the native populations. Large numbers of Han Chinese continue to be settled in both areas, diluting the percentage of original occupants. This relentless process has transformed significantly their basic character. Meanwhile the methods employed have become increasingly harsh. Both nations were always religious in character, a situation totally unacceptable to China's atheistic government. Currently at least two million Uyghur Muslims are imprisoned in massive concentration camps devoted to ideological indoctrination and various forms of repression. The limited information that is available confirms that systematic torture and brainwashing are widespread. It is apparent the ultimate objective in both Tibet and Xinjiang is nothing less than obliterating completely the resident populations. In this way any obstacle will be removed to the total incorporation of both areas into China. Essentially this means negating the historical fact that either country ever existed as an independent entity. This focus on "ethnic cleansing" is rooted in the pervasive belief within the Chinese government that the Han people are inherently superior and entitled to engage in any behavior - no matter how flagrant - that furthers this belief.

Recently the willingness of China to employ bold aggression to further its expansionist aspirations was demonstrated anew. Once again basic standards of law have been ignored as well as international public opinion. Without warning China has asserted control over the entire South China Sea, a large body of navigable water vital to global commerce. This unilateral claim includes all natural resources as well as the shipping lanes. With the loss of freedom of access to the area, the interests of nearby countries have been seriously comprised along with those of the entire world community.

The name "South China Sea" is largely a western formulation of recent origin and somewhat misleading. Over the centuries the area has been categorized in a variety of ways including that it is an extension of the Indian Ocean. The particular name that is chosen depends on the source. According to the Philippines the area is the "West Philippine Sea" and Vietnam the "East Sea." In the sixteenth century Portuguese traders employed the term "Cham Sea," and the Arabs the "Luzon Sea." Another longstanding name is "Clove Sea." While China alleges its claim rests on a firm historical basis, no such provable claim actually exists. As a result the Philippines disputed the matter before the United Nations Permanent Court of Arbitration in the Hague. The Court decided against China that has ignored the ruling completely, demonstrating anew its total disregard of equitable dealings when its interests are served. Over the years this has included a repeated willingness to void signed agreements as well as historical precedent itself.

This spurious claim over the South China Sea has been bolstered by constructing artificial islands on previously uninhabited atolls. Air force and naval bases along with missile batteries soon followed. On one atoll in the Spratly Island chain, a port larger than Pearl Harbor is nearing completion. These various bases provide a stepping stone to project Chinese power far into the western Pacific. All American bases (including Guam, Samoa and the Northern Mariana Islands) are now within reach of bombers flying from the newly constructed islands. An important corollary is undermining Taiwan's fragile independence.

This unilateral seizure of such a large body of international water has taken the global community completely by surprise. In spite of unanimous condemnation, China continues to solidify its position, responding belligerently when any attempt is made to enter the area. Thus the regime in Beijing has made clear its determination to challenge at any time the global order and alter at will established boundaries - in other words, grab whatever it wants. The tepid response by the world community has not been lost on China's leaders. Most nearby countries have grudgingly accepted the new status quo in order to avoid a direct dispute with their powerful neighbor.

In contrast to the overt seizure of the South China Sea, the Belt and Road project takes a more subtle approach. However, the objective is the same - facilitating China's control over important locations with strategic significance. Parallels are often drawn between the OBOR project and America's Marshall Plan, the vast "aid" program (a generous gift) that rebuilt Europe at the end of the World War II. Such a comparison is totally misleading. In contrast to the Marshall Plan, OBOR is subsidized almost completely on expensive credit. While many of the countries involved naively consider themselves fortunate to be included in such a grandiose undertaking, in every respect China is the big winner. Its engineers design the projects while Chinese companies and workers do the construction. Costly Chinese materials are used while banks controlled by China's government earn exorbitant interest. Ultimately the facility is managed on a permanent basis by Chinese personnel, who become quasi-independent residents with an ability to exert ongoing, political pressure. In essence, they represent a permanent fifth column that inevitably over time will erode the independence of the host nation - in other words transform it into a traditional colony disguised as something completely different.

An example is the tiny country of Laos at the core of strategic Southeast Asia. China has been building a 260 mile railroad system that connects eight, nearby countries. The estimated cost for Laos is $6 billion for a country whose total annual output is barely $12 billion. The project will never be self-sustaining but instead is rapidly becoming an insurmountable, financial burden. Soon Laos's public debt will reach 70% of GDP. Already at least 100,000 Chinese citizens are present there, a number that will likely grow, amounting over time to creeping annexation of the entire country. Because of its pivotal location, control of Laos leads potentially to dominance over the entire region. Laos adjoins Vietnam with which China is often at odds. In the event of armed conflict, the only country that is a significant obstacle to China's ambitions in the area would quickly find itself in an indefensible position.

Because of the large sums being loaned to participating countries, it is not surprising that a debt crises is erupting in many of them. On the tiny island nation of Sri Lanka at the center of the Indian Ocean, China has constructed a large port at Hambantota along with related facilities that include a sizeable airport. What is typically involved in some of these projects is not merely a port or docking facility but instead a large, self-sustaining facility with many capabilities that can include manufacturing as well.

Feasibility studies demonstrated that the port at Hambantota would never pay for itself. As a result Sri Lanka's debt load to Chinese companies (and hence China's government) rose rapidly to $8 billion - an astronomical sum for a tiny, island nation. After default, China took control of the port that is now available to its rapidly expanding navy. Thus in a relatively brief time a valuable, self-contained facility has been acquired at the heart of the Indian Ocean with a large number of Chinese citizens permanently residing there.

Once again the true implications of what seemed at first a promising arrangement have quickly manifested themselves. At this point it is possible that eventually Sri Lanka could lose its ability to function as an independent nation. An additional advantage for China is the fact Sri Lanka is situated only a short distance from the center of India's lengthy coastline. Thus without firing a shot, China has acquired the means to exert ongoing pressure on its longstanding foe.

On the strategic northeast coast of Africa ("Horn of Africa"), Djibouti is also falling rapidly under China's control. Chinese companies have constructed an important multipurpose port facility at Doraleh along with a $490 million electric railway connecting to Ethiopia. Aspiring to be a key transshipment point into the heart of Africa, Djibouti has acquired a debt load to Chinese companies that quickly escalated to over 80% of GDP. As a result China was granted the right to build a large, military facility not far from the port. It can be expected that eventually the two facilities will function as a single entity. In spite of its modest size, Djibouti's importance cannot be overstated. Its location in the northwest Indian Ocean dominates the southern route from the Gulf of Aden through the narrow Bab-el-Mandeb Strait to the Red Sea and onward to the Suez Canal. What is involved at this key location is the potential ability to dominate about one-quarter of global exports traveling by sea.

Also at Djibouti is a longstanding US base. Through the new facility Chinese personnel are able to monitor communications and most of what the American military is doing in the area. Since arriving there, they have also engaged in an ongoing campaign of harassment. This includes using high-powered lasers to interfere with military aircraft. It is apparent that China's ultimate objective is to gain sufficient influence over Djibouti's government so the US base is eliminated entirely.

Another small country falling into the China debt trap is Montenegro on the coast of the Adriatic Sea. Chinese companies have been constructing a highway extending from the port of Bar to landlocked Serbia. Because of the unsustainable costs, Montenegro's tax burden has increased rapidly. This has only slowed the escalating debt load to Chinese companies that already approaches 90% of GDP. From the start feasibility studies demonstrated that the project would likely become a crushing burden for a nation of only 600,000 inhabitants. In the likely event of forfeit, China will control an invaluable corridor to its longtime ally, Serbia, at the heart of the strategic Balkans. China is also building a high-speed rail link from Serbia to Hungary. It is well-known that Montenegro intends to seek membership in the European Union. Thus China will eventually control a route into the heart of the European Union that connects directly to its many, maritime assets in the area of the Indian Ocean.

Also of significance are recent developments in Pakistan, where China is acquiring an enormous strategic beachhead. Currently it is constructing the "Orange Line," an elaborate, elevated rail system in Lahore. This is the initial stage of a long-term $62 billion dollar scheme financed on expensive credit that is known as the "China-Pakistan Economic Corridor." Once again an overly ambitious, infrastructure project has quickly gotten into financial trouble with Pakistan seeking assistance from international sources. There is talk of substantial sums lost to bribes and corruption with much of the money not invested in any productive asset. This is another dark aspect of the Belt and Road scheme that no one speaks about. Most of the countries involved are dominated by small groups that are either corrupt or financially unsophisticated. As a result they agree to unrealistic projects involving large sums that can be easily diverted. Well aware of this unsavory fact, China's operatives lavish as much money as possible on such regimes. Ultimately the unpayable debt is the responsibility of the citizenry while a considerable portion of the money has gone elsewhere.

This insidious process is illustrated vividly in Pakistan, where there are reports of corruption on an unprecedented scale. Even China's cynical representatives are amazed by what they encountered. As a result it is anticipated that eventually control of the important port facility on the coast at Gwadar will end up in China's hands. Already it is managed by a Chinese company on a long-term lease. Not far away China is building a naval base at Jiwani, while the airfield near Turbat is being upgraded to accommodate heavy transport airplanes. Thus China will occupy a considerable portion of the entire peninsula in Pakistan's western Balochistan province next to its important, long-term ally Iran (a principal source of crude oil). Also of note a large facility will soon be constructed by

China on the island of Astola off the coast near Pakistan's naval base at Pasni. It will likely operate in an independent fashion where activities China wants to conceal will be conducted. It can be expected that some sort of missile system will be installed there that is similar to what has recently been constructed on atolls in the South China Sea. These various facilities in Pakistan represent a major coup for China and have enormous value for its rapidly expanding navy. There are indications that Pakistan will provide ongoing, logistical support as needed.

In this way China is rapidly assembling a large, well-coordinated offensive capability not far from the Strait of Hormuz, the route through which a large portion of oil for the West is transported. Iran and China have made no secret of the fact that the two countries work closely together. Iran's harassment activities in the Middle East further China's interests as well as its own. The close, working relationship between these two countries is demonstrated by the advanced weaponry suddenly possessed by Iran, especially of a naval character. This raises the issue of the large, cash pavements (one-half billion $US) from America given in recent years to the Iranian regime as a conciliatory gesture. It is likely that much of this money went to China in order to enhance Iran's military capabilities while undermining further US interests in the area.

During a time of crisis China now has the ability to

dominate to a significant extent both the strategic Arabian Sea and the northwest Indian Ocean. This includes protecting shipments of Iranian oil that are vital to China. Compounding the problem, Pakistan, America's one-time ally, has thrown in its lot with China. No doubt, the massive debt obligation has played a decisive role in this arrangement. As a result it can be expected that there will be increased conflict between Pakistan and India provoked by China against their longstanding, *mutual* foe.

The situation in Pakistan illustrates the complexity of China's long-term planning in connection with the OBOR project. Through an arrangement with Tajikistan in central Asia, a Chinese military base has been established in the eastern Gorno-Badakhshan Autonomous Region. This area adjoins Afghanistan's Badakhshan Province and the important Wakhan Corridor that connects to China. Of late, China has become a big investor in Afghanistan. Its position is enhanced by favorable relations with the Taliban insurgents presumed by many to be a Pakistan proxy. Having received large amounts of aid from the United States, Pakistan continues to play both sides against each other. In this volatile situation China cleverly presents itself as the peaceful, third party promoting various projects that really favor its own interests. These include a recently acquired 30-year lease on the valuable Aynak copper mine. Obviously China's ultimate goal is to exclude the U.S. entirely from Afghanistan so it has a completely free hand. Thus America's military forces will have waged a costly war for almost two decades with little to show for such a costly, longstanding effort.

Control of Afghanistan will enable China to link together its various assets throughout Central Asia including transport routes along with oil and gas pipelines. Afghanistan's enormous natural resources include large amounts of coal, gold, copper, natural gas, etc.. While appearing to be motivated by peaceful, economic cooperation, China is once again playing its strategic cards in the most advantageous way. With the China-Pakistan Economic Corridor extending all the way through Afghanistan into China, Chinese troops will have free movement directly to the shores of the Indian Ocean and the facilities being constructed there. The bases in Djibouti, Pakistan and Sri Lanka enable China to exert a virtual stranglehold on a large portion of the Indian Ocean. In addition, India is being placed in an increasingly vulnerable situation while the role of America's blue water navy in the area continues to be diminished.

Recently a particularly ominous situation developed in strategic South Africa, the dominant nation in sub-Sahara Africa. An avowed communist government with close ties to China has taken power on a radical agenda. This includes amending the constitution so the country's highly productive, white-owned farmland can be seized without compensation. Thus an important stabilizing force in the country's economy as well as a link to the western community will be eliminated.

At present South Africa has the only productive economy in the entire sub-Saharan region. The likely result of this bold land grab will duplicate the unfortunate experience in Zimbabwe. Years ago land seizures crippled the country's agricultural base that at one time fed a significant portion of the African continent. Subsequently Zimbabwe sank into poverty and became dependent on outside sources to survive. For obvious reasons this is exactly what China wants for South Africa.

It is apparent that the direction of the new communist government is being orchestrated by Chinese operatives. Upwards of 300 cadres of South African government officials are sent on a regular basis to mainland China for indoctrination in Marxist-Leninist theory. This will provide ideological justification for the eventual seizure by the government of "all" property in South Africa "in the name of the people." Ultimately the rapidly growing strategic linkage between China and South Africa will impact the entire African continent. The expropriation process in South Africa will not end with white farmers, many of whom have already been murdered or fled the country. The objective is to isolate the country from the West so it is increasingly dependent on China for funding, technical assistance and ideological guidance. Thus South Africa will become a showcase Marxist-Leninist state serving as an example for the rest of Africa. Potentially the entire continent could become a giant colony serving Chinese interests. In nearby Tanzania a similar effort to spread Marxist ideology and hence Chinese influence is underway. In Zimbabwe China is constructing an underground, military base to house large numbers of special forces, who can be moved rapidly around the continent. Already missile batteries are stationed at various locations in Zimbabwe that will enhance China's dominance of the country along with the entire southern continent.

Throughout Africa China has already entered into longstanding, loan agreements related to a large portion of the continent's valuable natural resources. This is especially true of metals with military and high-tech applications. Also important is unfettered access to unspoiled farmland. Through rampant pollution related to industrialization, China has destroyed much of its own farmland. As a result it is dependent for food on many, foreign nations, including the United States - a situation that is totally unacceptable to the communists. Sub-Sahara Africa provides the perfect alternative, especially because there are so many weak regimes ripe for dominance by a much larger and powerful nation.

Similar to the pattern employed elsewhere, many countries in Africa are heavily indebted to Chinese banks that repeatedly extend additional, expensive credit. If future events continue in the same direction, the result is inevitable. Thus dependency is spreading rapidly throughout Africa with China successfully presenting itself as the generous friend decrying the legacy of western colonialism. At all times its operatives portray themselves as motivated by supposedly humane Marxist ideology focused on assisting the disadvantaged peoples of the Third World. Needless to say, the systematic abuses perpetrated by China's government on its own citizens are never mentioned

Chinese telecom company Transsion Holdings has even designed an inexpensive smart phone that is expected to monopolize mobile communications throughout Africa. This opens the door to a variety of services provided by other companies fronting for the Chinese government. In this way virtually all communications on the continent could be monitored and controlled. As this process of creeping aggression in the name of economic cooperation continues to spread, a potentially unpleasant future lies ahead for the African continent. This is especially true of the people of South Africa, who don't appreciate the true character of those they view now as allies. Ultimately China will not bring a bright economic future but instead one of unmitigated bleakness.

In South America a similar situation is developing although at a slower pace. Once again numerous, high-cost infrastructure projects and commodity purchase agreements have been funded through the usual, overly generous loans. In this way large portions of the continent's resources (including copper, soybeans iron ore, etc.) are tied up for an indefinite period. This is especially true of petroleum. In Ecuador, China controls 90% of the country's production far into the future.

All of this has been accomplished in a relatively brief time by cultivating relationships with leftist presidents in countries such as Venezuela, Bolivia, Uruguay, Brazil and Argentina.

Venezuela is a prime example. Possessing huge oil reserves, it was at one time the envy of the entire continent. After years of "socialist" mismanagement, this once-prosperous country has been driven completely into ruin with many of its citizens fleeing to other countries to avoid starvation. Recently a five billion dollar loan was arranged with China that supplements other financial arrangements propping up the corrupt, government. With the recent financial bailout, the country is almost totally dependent on China and Russia for survival while linked closely to communist Cuba. The government of Venezuela has even hired the Chinese company ZTE to design a monitoring system similar to the draconian Social Credit Score in China. Supposedly it will be tied to ration cards required for food and include a variety of criteria related to personal behavior. That was before food supplies in the country were exhausted. Having experienced the initial stage of so-called "socialism" and its inevitable consequences, *Venezuela is following the usual route leading inevitably to collapse and communist rule with its citizens losing all control over their destiny.*

In that regard it is important to note China's growing influence in Jamaica only a short distance from the Florida coast. Of late, Beijing has invested heavily in the small island nation. This includes purchasing the Alpart aluminum refinery and also building an important toll road recently taken over by a Chinese company. In the capital of Kingston, China has been constructing several road projects - the cost an astronomical $89 billion dollars. In addition, the link between Kingston and Port San Antonio on the northeast coast is being upgraded. With Jamaica's debt continuing to escalate rapidly, a crushing burden has been acquired by this tiny nation with a limited economy focused largely on tourism.

China's economic influence is spreading rapidly throughout the entire Caribbean with large sums loaned to a total of nine island nations. In addition, close ties of various sorts, including military, are being promoted with all of these small but strategic nations that are becoming increasingly dependent on China. Recently Chinese naval vessels have been observed near Venezuela. It can be expected that soon an attempt will be made to construct a major military base somewhere in the Caribbean as American interests continue to be undermined to a dangerous degree.

Meanwhile most government officials throughout South America eagerly embrace China's assistance while viewing with admiration its accomplishments as a fellow Third World country. As a result they continue to participate in projects that promote Chinese interests. Recently Argentina granted China a key location in the mountains where a large, satellite listening station is being erected. Supposedly the purpose is peaceful, scientific research, although the facility actually provides a highly effective means of monitoring all America's satellite communications, especially military.

A particularly serious situation has developed regarding both Panama and Mexico. The strategic Panama Canal is vital to global commerce as well as the movement of US naval vessels between the Atlantic and Pacific Oceans. In 1999 the government of Panama took complete control of this vital waterway. The advisability of this overly generous divestiture has long been questioned. Recently *China acquired the port facilities at Cristobal and Balboa so it effectively dominates access to the canal at both ends. Thus the United States has to a large extent lost control of this vital maritime link that it constructed at such enormous cost.* The movement of America's navy between the Atlantic and Pacific can now be impeded so potentially its vessels will one day have to utilize the lengthy route around the tip of South America. With China's influence in Argentina growing rapidly, this alternate route at some point might also be compromised.

The two, ports controlling access to the canal were acquired by Hutchinson Whampoa, a front company closely connected to China's PLA. To make matters worse, nearby facilities that once belonged to the US military have also fallen under PLA control. Furthermore additional ports on Mexico's Pacific coast are also controlled by Hutchinson Whampoa - Manzanillo and the Ensenada International Terminal that is only 65 miles from the porous US border. Typically the use of covert operatives is fundamental to China's military theory, and it is only reasonable to assume that such individuals are embedded in the resident populations at both of these locations. As a result spies and saboteurs can at any time be funneled easily into the US heartland.

In sum, the Chinese military has acquired at little expense a vast, overseas intelligence network, especially at the most strategic locations related to international transport. In this regard the significance of COSCO, the huge, shipping container company should be noted. Its containers are literally everywhere on land and sea and even on railroads throughout America. What is not appreciated is that the company is controlled by the logistics department of the People's Liberations Army. It has been determined that a newly designed cruise missile system can be concealed and fired from such containers.

An important development of recent vintage is the addition of armed, security groups at the various sites of the Belt and Road Project. Portrayed as supposedly peaceful "security personnel," this well-trained, global force is controlled by China's infamous Ministry of Public Security, the key governmental group at the heart of the Chinese police state. If the security of resident workers was the only issue, it would not be necessary to involve an organization focused on the worst sort of coercive behavior. Essentially these so-called security groups constitute in the aggregate an embedded, heavily armed force that is literally everywhere on the globe. There is little constraint on the size of these forces, the true purpose of which is easily concealed. In time of war they will be able to initiate a variety of aggressive actions, even occupying nearby territory and sabotaging the commercial and military assets of other countries. It is obvious why China places so much emphasis on facilities at or near so-called global "chokepoints," a name that is highly appropriate considering their significance.

In southeast Asia China is investing heavily in eleven infrastructure projects in Malaysia with two, important ports on the west coast coming under Chinese dominance. Both are on the shore of the vital Strait of Malacca through which 40 % of the world's global shipping passes. Thus *in time of war China currently possesses the ability to dominate to a significant degree all of the world's most important naval chokepoints. This includes the Panama Canal, Strait of Hormuz, Strait of Malacca, and the Suez Canal through the Bar-el-Mandeb Strait.*

In the western Pacific several, tiny island nations are situated in nearly eight million miles of strategic, maritime space. Among others they include the Marshall and Solomon Islands, Nauru, Paulau, Tonga, etc.. It is an area vital to global peace as well as the free movement of American naval forces in the Pacific. Relying largely on cyclical tourism, these tiny nations currently owe China over $1.3 billion dollars in high-interest credits they cannot service. This opens the door to land seizures or other punitive arrangements. Not surprising, there are reports that China aspires to establish a large military base in the area. Supplementing the newly created bases in the South China Sea, this would provide China with the means to dominate the entire western Pacific region and potentially the approaches to Hawaii itself.

In sum, Chinese front companies currently control more than 60 strategically located ports and terminals around the globe. Among others, the countries involved include Djibouti, Sri Lanka, Pakistan, Egypt, Morocco, Myanmar, Cambodia, Indonesia, Israel, Spain, Italy Belgium, Cote d'Ivoire, Mexico, Panama, Brazil and even Australia. In Europe China has acquired a significant or dominant position in 13 ports and controls completely the historically important port of Piraeus in Greece. Some of these facilities have been acquired by outright purchase at above market prices, thus accelerating the rapid growth of the system. As the OBOR project continues to spread rapidly, the true significance of this growing system of ports and terminals is becoming increasingly apparent. *Because of their location and how they interconnect, these facilities afford China the ability in time of war to undermine the freedom of movement of a large portion of global society.*

An underlying theme throughout this process of subtle but relentless encroachment is China's preoccupation with thwarting America's blue water navy and its role stabilizing the international order. Also it is the only military force that can oppose China's escalating ambitions on the high seas. As noted, China continues to establish a growing foothold in South Africa that likely will soon include a naval facility on the coast. This could be used to dominate traffic around the strategic Horn of Africa - the gateway between the Atlantic and Indian Oceans. In conjunction with what has happened with the Panama Canal, the inability to pass freely around the tip of Africa would undermine further the effectiveness of America's navy as a global force.

The maritime environment of the Indian Ocean impacts directly the entire Asian continent. This will be especially true in time of war. Through land corridors leading to Pakistan and Myanmar, China now has the ability to move sizeable military forces rapidly to the shores of the Indian Ocean and from there to various locations including those in Africa. As a result America's role in the area continues to be minimized, a situation highly damaging to long-term, Western interests.

<u>All</u> Chinese commercial, maritime vessels are constructed according to strict, military specifications that include being armed heavily. Although appearing otherwise, these vessels are really a huge, offensive, naval force currently located in key ports and waterways throughout the world. Hence they are available at all times for the rapid transport of personnel and materials to disputed areas and even for

disruptive, military operations. In addition, they can coordinate with the armed personnel already stationed at China's various ports or infrastructure facilities.

Truly the obsessive leaders in Beijing think on a very large and dangerous scale. Their purposeful megalomania is monumental in character as well as remarkably effective. While the global community continues to underestimate what is taking place in plain view, China's propagandists criticize the West for its imperialist history - a theme adopted by many in the Third World and even among some intellectuals and politicians in America. In fact, China's 21st century version of colonialism disguised as economic cooperation dwarfs anything that transpired in the past. The implications for global peace and the future survival of the democratic West are obvious. It is ironic that what little money China has expended on the project and the enormous tactical advantages it provides comes for the most part from the United States through endless, one-sided commercial arrangements.

In sum, the OBOR project viewed by many as "globalization" at its best is something totally different - a far-reaching scheme intended to create a network of economic-based, <u>military bases </u>that spans the globe. It is ironic that the system is being subsidized largely by many of the host nations, that are literally paying for the privilege of eventually losing some or all of their sovereignty With sophisticated, armed personnel, spies and saboteurs embedded at these sites (including those not far from the American border), China's has established a global presence the significance of which cannot be overstated.

At any time these resident forces dispersed around the world can initiate a variety of aggressive actions that include asserting control over vital land and sea passageways. Thus it will be possible to suppress or shut down for a significant period freedom of movement almost anywhere in the world. This ingenious scheme masquerading as economic cooperation is a key component of China's far-reaching quest for global dominance, the implications of which will eventually manifest themselves in terms even more overt.

THE GREAT CHINA SCAM

4

With its influence spreading rapidly around the entire globe, the communist regime in China also dominates many, important industries along with the supply of key, raw materials. This escalating power extends deep into the American economy itself. While long ago major portions of the domestic manufacturing base were transferred to the Far East, financial "buyouts" have enabled some of the most prominent US corporations to be acquired by operatives of the Chinese government. This includes key sectors of high-technology, communications, entertainment (movies) and even transport. In essence, this broad-based power exercised by a hostile, foreign state is assuming such an invasive character that eventually it could undermine America's independence as a sovereign nation. The question is how could a once-impoverished, Third World nation have acquired so much unchecked power and do so in such a brief period. The answer can be referred to appropriately as the "Great China Scam."

Only a generation ago China was a backward country lacking technology and capital, the key ingredients needed to build a modern society. At the time no one could have imagined the transformation that lay ahead or how quickly it would occur. In fact, it was reasonable to assume that the rise of China to the status of a global power would take the better part of a century. For much of its history the country's principal asset was its enormous, hard-working population that could not be fed properly, an almost insurmountable obstacle to rapid progress. Nonetheless, over such a limited period China has been transformed into a powerful, advanced nation asserting itself aggressively on every front. It is an extraordinary achievement. In the annals of history nothing similar has happened and likely will never be duplicated. The way all of this has been accomplished is the most compelling aspect of this unique story and also the most troubling. *In essence, China's remarkable progress has been achieved by perpetrating on the rest of the world an ingenious "Ponzi" scheme of extraordinary scope.*

Early in the 1980s the regime headed by Deng Xiaoping (Mao Zedong's immediate successor) accelerated the timetable for China's development by formulating a far-reaching economic plan to undermine and ultimately displace the nations of the democratic West. The key elements are *"deception" and deceitfulness on a grand scale adapted to the realm of economics.* In this way the world's dominant powers would be tricked into subsidizing China's rise. Anything of importance that couldn't be acquired in any other way would be stolen and, if necessary, in the most flagrant way. Over the years numerous agreements have been signed by China and promptly broken. Always the objective is manipulating the global community into serving China's interests. In sum, for decades the world's most populous nation has been motivated exclusively by double-dealing and trickery on a monumental scale - a cynical undertaking the success of which has exceeded anything the strategists of China could have hoped for.

All of this was accomplished by disguising the real objectives behind the appealing image of a supposedly misunderstood, Third World country eager to be a reliable partner on economic matters. In addition, the empty hope was fostered that eventually trade would bring democracy to China - something particularly appealing to Americans. In other words, because of the benefits of economic cooperation, the hard-liners in Beijing would supposedly abandon their global ambitions and willingly hand over power to their fellow citizens whom they have victimized in the worst way. Not surprising, this naïve notion was from the start a clever fiction intended to distract attention from the real objectives being pursued. To this day the country remains the direct opposite of what the compliant capitalists were tricked into believing. It has not democratized to the slightest degree but instead only grown even more authoritarian while at the same time becoming a major threat to global peace.

In reality China's much-admired economy (so-called "Red Capitalism") is nothing more than an elaborate façade - literally an ingenious "Potemkin" village behind which the government conceals its all-pervasive and controlling role. Although there are semi-independent "businessmen" with a degree of freedom, they always act within the parameters set by the government. In essence, they are nothing more than compliant "straw men" held on a tight leash. For their efforts they have been rewarded handsomely, and many are quite rich. Still China's business community is not independent in any true sense but instead the highly motivated agents of a dictatorial authority. In this way a benign face has been placed on the accelerating rise of a repressive regime determined to address longstanding, historical grievances and one day demonstrate the inherent superiority of the Han people.

Equally important, every aspect of China's controlled economy is tied in one way or another to its ambitious military. All along America's business and financial communities have been duped into being unwitting partners with the regime's focal point and power center - the People's Liberation Army (PLA). In this way decades of so-called peaceful interaction have enabled China's military to become the dangerous force it is today. This ominous situation is only possible because of the wealth and technology acquired under false pretenses from the West. So much for the growth of democracy through trade, a naive notion that will go down in history as one of the greatest errors of collective judgment of all time. It is ironic that a key reason for the success of this extraordinary scheme is the desire of the world's democracies to foster cooperation and openness - an admirable trait the communists have exploited in every, possible way. Thus something laudable has been transformed into a form of weakness. Although such cynicism is reprehensible in the extreme, it has served the communists' objectives perfectly and achieved exactly what they want.

The inspiration for this far-reaching scheme is rooted in China's past, outlined 25 centuries ago in the revered classic of Oriental culture - Sun Tzu's *Art of War*. In the quest for power the key element of "deception" is always the dominant consideration. This is a concept the nations of the West have difficulty understanding because it runs counter to the principles on which they are based. The only significant difference from Sun Tzu's thinking is the modern context as well as the scale of what it involved. Unfortunately the world's democracies fail to realize that all along they have been engaged in an undeclared war that precedes a much larger conflict still to come. Needless to say, it has not been in the communists' interests to clarify their true intentions.

Who would have thought that a weak, vulnerable nation would undertake such an audacious program? Nonetheless the communists have succeeded to an extraordinary degree, and it has changed history. In fact, one cannot overstate the value of what's been lost or more to the point stolen, and all of this has been accomplished with relative ease. What is difficult to understand is how completely the global, business community has allowed itself to be deceived. It might be thought that such a description unfairly misrepresents the situation. In fact, it understates what has happened as well as the gravity of what lies in the future.

Those devoted to the art of the "scam" always dream of a scheme that proves they're true masters of the art. Just go to Las Vegas and in the dimly lit bars listen to the conversations among the hustlers and weirdoes hunched over their drinks. Hope springs eternal in the hearts of true con men and those who aspire to be one. With most scams, however, things rarely work out as expected, and in the end the only ones conned are the con men themselves. But this time it was different, and the biggest rip-off of the ages worked just as it was planned. The clever commissars of China thought this one through and then some, and although shooting for the moon, got it just right. In fact, it worked out better than any of them could have imagined in their wildest dreams.

In this regard one might recall the inimitable Bernie Madoff and others like him of recent vintage. As you may recall, Bernie's $50 billion hustle targeted lots of gullible, rich people, who afterwards weren't so rich. In comparison to what the communists in China have achieved, Bernie and all the others are strictly bush league. Another relevant point - with the Great China Scam many of the people who have been ticked in the worst way are those with advanced degrees in economics and business. Supposedly it's only little guys with a lunch pail who get fleeced and not those with fancy credentials. Not this time.

To be blunt about the matter, it's clear the communists have come to view the international business community as a bunch of fancy "marks" they can easily manipulate, and that's exactly what they've achieved. After so many years the same thing keeps happening again and again. Unfortunately many in business and finance will always have difficulty accepting the fact that along with the rest of us they've been taken completely to the cleaners. Nonetheless, what China has achieved is the ultimate scam that in its details constitutes history's most successful "Ponzi" scheme. It just proves that if you concoct the right fantasy about lots of easy money, almost anyone can be taken. Human nature never changes, and what's too good to be true usually is. Meanwhile the clever cons in Beijing, who have literally outsmarted the world, keep pulling the strings even tighter while laughing all the way to the bank of global supremacy.

Of late, there have been so many rip-offs in the financial realm it seems that anything is possible when it comes to large amounts of money. This period is one for the books alright - the great age of hyper-speculation of every type and variety and then some. Of course, the people involved are only demonstrating how creative they can be, and at times the rewards have been huge. Unfortunately along the way some very unfortunate things have happened that usually involve a bizarre, financial instrument. For instance, there are the ones built on "guaranteed to fail mortgage loans" that nearly wrecked the global housing market. No doubt, some of you remember that masterpiece because it may have caused you to lose your home and now you're reading this book in a small room at the local YMCA. In essence, we're living in the era preoccupied with maximizing monetary value while often ignoring basic, ethical considerations. For instance, a way was found to rig ("influence") LIBOR (the most important interest rate) and also key components of the foreign exchange system (the world's biggest, financial market). Things like that aren't supposed to happen. Also let's not forget all those ingenious "derivatives" currently available through your local, financial conglomerate. They should really be called high-class "wagers" because that's what derivatives are. Although some serve a legitimate hedging purpose that's improved certain aspects of the investment world, many have little constructive purpose. Not surprising, such arrangements are often so complicated that hardly anyone can understand them. Of course, that's the point. The only thing apparent to the party on the other end is that they keep losing even more money. In an environment like this it was inevitable that compliments of China's so-called communists the global community would be afforded the privilege of being collectively fleeced by the most elaborate and cynical, economic scheme of all time.

Another relevant factor: the great China Scam has been dignified by its connection to the dominant, theme of global economics for a generation. For those with limited information about the subject, so-called "globalization" is the free movement across national boundaries of technology, labor and capital in order to link the world more closely. As a result everyone is supposed to work together more effectively. In theory all of this sounds quite enlightened and in some respects it is. Although this grand, economic experiment with political overtones has been tried before, it was never on such a comprehensive scale. While the current version is generally considered a noteworthy success, not everyone would agree. This includes the large numbers of American workers who have experienced a significantly reduced standard of living. That happened because so many of their jobs were taken by the legions of low-paid workers in faraway places like China.

It's ironic that this progressive, economic theme of recent decades would pave the way for China to pursue its cynical, national agenda. In fact, the deception perpetrated by China can be viewed appropriately as a perverse offshoot of globalization - in essence, elaborate theft posing as international cooperation. While some are still convinced America's relationship with China is a noteworthy success, they fail to recognize the fact that every year a significant portion of America's most valuable intellectual property continues to be stolen along with huge amounts of our national wealth. At the same time many prominent corporations have succeeded in squandering their company's hard-earned competitive position in China. Thus a severe blow has been dealt to the future of all

Americans. And don't forget the many jobs that went out the door. Perhaps someday they'll return, or at least that's the hope.

Meanwhile a competing, industrial base has been created on a foreign shore that's subsidizing a massive war machine currently threatening world peace. In essence, *leading figures in global business, finance and government have inadvertently aided the creation of an entity that embodies the worst nightmare of the democratic West*. Of course, it's laudable that so many in America want to think positively about other countries and help them prosper. As a result a lot of naïve assumptions continue to be made about China that simply aren't true. Now much of the harm that's been caused can never be undone. And all of this happened because of a run-of-the-mill but very clever "Ponzi" scheme executed on a grand scale that's outfoxed lots of very smart people who should have known better.

Also worth noting is the fact the Great China Scam wasn't thought up by some well-heeled guys who look like they just stepped out of a top men's fashion magazine. Probably none of Deng Xiaoping's cronies ever owned a business suit, an expensive briefcase or even a silk tie. It just shows that if you set up the right con connected to lots of easy money, that's all that matters. Now this scheme *extraordinaire* will forever represent the gold standard for the hustlers and weirdoes dreaming away in all those dimly lit Las Vegas bars –

that is, when they learn how ingenious the whole thing really is.

For those unacquainted with the subterfuge known as a "Ponzi scheme," the basic details are quite simple. The first step is to fashion some sort of irresistible illusion connected to money and lots of it. As a result those considered the "marks" won't be able to resist playing the game that's designed to deceive them. Although no guarantees are given, they comply nonetheless because the "bait" is so enticing it convinces them they can't lose. That's where the art comes in. The marks have to believe without reservation because you identified the right illusion that will deceive them. Not everyone can pull off a successful Ponzi scheme so don't underestimate how difficult it is.

Incidentally the term, "Ponzi scheme" originated in the early 1920s with a Boston businessman turned hustler named Charles Ponzi. Briefly Charles was so successful in his newly adopted calling that now he's permanently associated with this particular form of devious behavior. In fact, many of the same components are present in all schemes intended to separate people from their hard-earned funds. This includes entire nations and their propensity at times for collective gullibility. The additional element that distinguishes Mr. Ponzi's noteworthy achievement is the skillful use of the mark's own money to sustain the illusion. As a result they keep handing over even more. In this way the marks continue to be manipulated while not realizing it's really their money being returned to them. In this regard the Great China Scam has achieved its most noteworthy success or more appropriately deception. All along this elaborate, international game has been played for the most part with the vast amounts of money drained inexorably out of America.

The focus of the grand deception fashioned by the communists is the world's last, untapped commercial market (China) and the enormous profits that supposedly can be earned there - that conveniently are just waiting to be taken by the supposedly astute. This is the allure that few businessmen in the West have been able to resist. Unfortunately from the start the game was rigged to defeat them. In other words no matter how compliant the outsiders have been, it's been a losing deal from the start. In fact, one can compare doing business in China to playing the table games in a rigged casino. Remember that if something is too good to be true, it usually is. Once again this enduring truism has been demonstrated in modern-day China. In fact, the extent to which the outsiders have been ripped off may never be fully realized or at least until it's too late. *Eventually every last dime invested directly or indirectly in China will be lost when all private property is confiscated.* That's the bitter, little pill the communists are holding in reserve. At this point time is growing shorter before it's finally dropped into the fatal, witches brew.

The supposed benefits dangled before the foreigners are

two-fold: access to an enormous, untapped marketplace variously estimated at almost 1.5 billion supposedly eager consumers; and secondly, an abundance of inexpensive products for importation back to their own countries. You must admit that on the surface all of this sounds quite promising. In order to take advantage of this allegedly fantastic deal, it was necessary for the global, business community to construct an industrial base in China. Of course, these facilities were financed mostly from the outside. In this way the US obtained at bargain basement prices lots of inexpensive consumer products such as sneakers, cell phones and the flat-screen TVs on which Americans love to watch sporting events. Meanwhile China's unlimited, consumer market never materialized - at least not to the extent everyone expected. That's because the communists don't want the bulk of their citizens to become prosperous. Otherwise they can't be controlled. Ultimately all those fancy sneakers and TV's proved to be a lot more expensive than anyone imagined.

Not surprising, the principal target of this ingenious scheme is the United States and its considerable wealth. As a result the most conspicuous feature has been the massive, ongoing trade deficit between China and America that on an annual basis averages around 400 billion $US and sometimes even more. That's a "4" followed by <u>eleven</u> very real zeros - an enormous amount, especially because it accumulates each and every year. *The importance to the communists of this huge, ongoing, trade deficit with the United States cannot be overstated. All along it's been the focus and indispensable component of their entire scheme. Without it the Great China Scam and everything built upon it would have never succeeded.* Over the last quarter century this totally rigged situation has provided China with the means to modernize its economy; build up a massive military; and also buy valuable assets all over the world. Now China has moved on to the logical, next step - gradually taking control of the economies of the nations that provided all of this wealth, especially the United States.

The enormous size of the trade deficit has been abetted by various factors guaranteeing that under any circumstances China can't lose. *The most important is an exchange rate rigged in favor of the "yuan" that's always "pegged" at an artificially low value to the US dollar. Consequently every transaction that passes between the two countries leads to the accumulation of even more wealth at America's expense.* In addition, a vast array of internal tariffs along with assorted, unfair business practices keep competing products out of China or make them so expensive they don't sell. Also most components of China's industrial base are state-owned and therefore subsidized and controlled by the government. As a result they operate internally and externally at an enormous advantage. Thus a US company competing with a China-based company is actually competing against the limitless resources of a national government.

If all of that isn't enough, it's necessary for foreign

businessmen entering China's market to share their technology with a mandatory Chinese "partner." You read that correctly. In order to be fortunate enough to do business in China, you have to partner with one of the government's carefully chosen representatives, who have no other interest except to expropriate everything you own and then some. Thus what took decades to develop is handed over on a silver platter - the Chinese getting all of it for next to nothing. If that sounds like a questionable deal, it certainly is. When most people hear about it for the first time, they think it's a joke. Unfortunately the joke is on the outsiders, especially the Americans, who even now continue to play this incredibly losing game. It's not surprising that so many foreign enterprises have lost their ability to compete and even fallen into Chinese hands. Others simply leave China with a very big hole in their pocket. There is one exception - a small number of large corporations with lots of political clout in their own countries. In general, these companies have done well. For now it's in the interests of the communists to keep them around, especially if they have additional, high-value technology that can be stolen.

Another relevant consideration is that the factories built in China employ Chinese workers and managers, who are, of course, closely connected to the mandatory partner or governmental representative. Not surprising, this has accelerated the loss of western technology. Eventually most of this know-how ends up in the hands of entrepreneurs also connected to the government, who respond by trying to put the foreigners out of business. As a result the communists have saved themselves decades of painstaking research, and they got all of it for next to nothing. It's been for them a fantastic deal, and not surprising they constantly extol the benefits of globalization, free trade and so-called "peaceful" international cooperation. As you may realize by now, as far as the communists are concerned, there is no such thing as a level or fair playing field. To add insult to injury, they have repeatedly signed agreements affording China the full benefits of the World Trade Organization while constantly undermining its basic principles. What all of this demonstrates is the power of the legendary Chinese market of so-called unlimited profits to warp the judgment of people who normally think in a very sober way.

Another relevant consideration and an important one - *a regime such as communist China only consumes capital or wealth. Like all totalitarian governments, it is inherently parasitic and functions by exploiting its own people and environment while skillfully using others to underwrite its partisan goals and inherent corruption.* Although in recent years communist China has provided a significant stimulus to the global economy, it has all along been feeding off the rest of the world like a gigantic leech. Each year it grows ever larger with a bigger appetite for foreign money in order to further its partisan agenda. Meanwhile the greatest Ponzi scheme of all times perpetuates itself with the astute Americans and others continuing to underwrite this wasteful process. While being drawn ever deeper into an enormous trap, many in the international business community are still incapable of comprehending how completely the world at large has been conned.

Before Deng Xiaoping and his cronies thought up the Great China Scam, the initial seed capital relied on by the communists was the enormous pool of savings set aside by the hard-working Chinese people. All of this money was deposited in government-owed banks so it was easily expropriated. Eventually this original pool of funds was exhausted so it was necessary to find a new source. That's when the eager foreigners entered the picture. They even obliged by purchasing much of the useless debt that had been dumped into so-called "bad banks." These banks were bad alight, although that didn't prevent the foreigners from lining up to play the losing game.

At the same time the assurance was made that eventually China's economy would open up completely, and fortunate for the communists the visitors bought into that illusion as well. They still do. The rest is history with the American trade deficit providing an ongoing source of funds so massive it can't be exhausted no matter how much is stolen or misused. That is until recently.

As noted, the international business community created an industrial base in China to take advantage of the country's enormous labor force that works for modest wages. Hence the low price of the consumer goods imported into countries like the United States. China's citizens from mostly rural areas benefited because of the jobs that were created. Basically such workers perform two, repetitive functions on an enormous scale - "stitching" clothes and "soldering" and assembling electronic devices. As you know, these mundane activities have little appeal for people in more advance countries. The latter task (soldering and assembling) is the more significant. The valuable components involved in modern electronic equipment are shipped to China where final assembly occurs. Therefore China is the point of exit for the finished product. While contributing the least sophisticated aspect of the overall process, China nonetheless obtains what many consider the most significant benefit from a trade standpoint.

Unfortunately it has been determined that often the finished, electronic products coming out of China contain some sort of embedded spyware. Since Chinese authorities place so much emphasis on espionage, this should not come as a surprise to anyone. Unfortunately some of the legions of tainted, computer mother boards have ended up in equipment used by major corporations and even the US government and military. For instance, one prominent US company had to discard over 7000 servers that were compromised. Obviously there wasn't much of a cost saving on that one. But as you may realize by now, China always comes out the big winner in any arrangement.

While such mundane procedures (stitching and soldering) underlie much of the ongoing trade deficit, this process also facilitates the continued theft of intellectual property. The presumed benefit for corporate America has been the ability to increase sales and short-term profits and hence the value of corporate stock. It's obvious that China and the outsiders take a very different approach. The communist regime emphasizes the long-term and consequently continues to outmaneuver their "guests" in every way. Meanwhile vast areas of America's once great, industrial heartland continue to sink ever deeper into ruin while the massive trade deficit enables China to buy up even more of the world's most valuable assets.

As noted, a key aspect of every successful Ponzi scheme is the clever use of the mark's own money to keep alive the illusion they're benefiting from the one-sided arrangement. In this regard China uses a small portion of the money acquired from the deficit to purchase America's most advanced products so eventually they can be reverse-engineered. Most of the proceeds, however, have been used to purchase an enormous cache of U.S. Treasury bonds and bills - indebtedness that future generations of Americans are obligated to pay. In this way all of us are now heavily indebted to this once-backward country that in reality has a very strong dislike of the US and everything it stands for.

As you can see, it's impossible to compete in a fair way with China. Obviously the trade deficit wouldn't be so large or even exist if the foreigners were given a fair deal. It is the combination of so many adverse factors that have enabled China to accumulate the vast pool of wealth that underwrites the objective to become the dominant, global power.

In sum, the ominous entity that currently is communist China is to a large extent the unfortunate creation of the democratic West. Without all the technology and wealth handed over so generously, the threat represented by modern-day China and its military would not exist. It's no accident that many of the repressive tools used to control the country's citizenry are derived from western technology. Furthermore, many ordinary Americans have eagerly invested in various aspects of the so-called China "miracle." As previously stated, every dollar invested there - either directly or indirectly - will eventually be lost or go to zero. While China amended its constitution to respect private property, that privilege can be revoked at will, which is exactly what's happened to so-called freedom of religion. When a major war breaks out, the nationalization of all private assets in China will be one of the first steps to be taken. This also includes what belongs to China's allegedly prosperous middle class. Along with the rest of us, they will also be taken to the all-time cleaners as a reward for their years of service helping the regime deceive the gullible foreigners. It's not surprising that so many of them smell a rat and are trying to get out of the country with at least some of their money - something that of late is easier said than done.

As the economic interdependence between the US and China becomes even more pervasive, the question arises whether the US can ever break free of such a stifling situation. This includes a growing Chinese presence in almost every aspect of the domestic economy. Especially important is stopping the financial hemorrhaging rooted in the trade deficit. The effort to reduce the deficit unilaterally has been denounced by many, "enlightened" commentators as short-slighted and even the equivalent of launching a trade war. It is not surprising that China keeps manipulating its currency in order to cancel the effects of any tariffs. Meanwhile lots of self-indulgent rhetoric regarding so-called free trade continues to emanate from Beijing. To this day few in America understand the clever game that China continues to play with such success - a monumental error of judgment that ultimately will have consequences more significant than what has already occurred. In essence, because of America's misguided preoccupation with short-term profits, China has acquired the ability to challenge the very existence of the democratic West.

From the start the regime in China faced a particularly difficult problem in its quest to construct what masquerades as a modern economy. A top-tier nation in international commerce must be represented by a currency that others are willing accept. Not long ago the "yuan" belonged to that unfortunate group of currencies most people try to avoid. A promising business deal can flounder because an undesirable currency is involved. The communists were fortunate to have a readily available way to solve this problem as well. As you might expect, it once again involves the trade deficit with America.

Payment for exports return to China in the form of US dollars - the world's reserve currency. (90% of all transactions in the $5.1 trillion dollar foreign exchange market involve US currency.) These valuable dollars returning to China are exchanged for yuan (referred to locally as renminbi), which are released internally. The People's Bank of China (the government) retains the dollars, which are used as foreign exchange and also as the huge, financial reserve invested largely in US government securities. It is this reserve that has played such a significant role validating the yuan. Without such backing, the current status of China's currency would have never been achieved.

After being exchanged for dollars, the yuan released into the Chinese economy are multiplied by the fractional banking system. This large pool of money provides ongoing stimulus. Like any government China can print as much of its national currency as desired. However, at a certain point this spawns inflation weakening the currency and the economy. Thanks to the generous pool of dollars positioned in US securities this problem has also been avoided.

Although there are institutions referred to as banks and insurance companies in China, that's not what they really are. Instead they are fully owned entities that form a tightly controlled network facilitating the internal movement of money on the government's behalf. In this way the regime is able to micro-manage every aspect of China's economic life. The illusion of a quasi-independent financial system has been essential to maintaining the false image of China's allegedly modern economy. In essence, *the financial system is nothing more than another clever illusion among so many others that encourages foreigners to play the phony game in China.*

Also the yuan's enhanced status was a key factor encouraging foreigners from around the world to invest in the country. All of this has contributed to the impressive but manipulated growth statistics China is so proud of. With the yuan more respected in international commerce, China has also become the world's great "money laundry" - a bizarre situation that has increased considerably the flow of funds in and out of the country. About one-quarter of all money floating around the globe emanates from a grey or black source. In other words no one really knows where it comes from. This, of course, is fine with the people who control this money. Some are criminals such as drug dealers, although the bulk of these funds emanate from corrupt politicians stealing from their own countries. After this money enters and leaves China, it is impossible to determine the initial source. As a result China continues to function as the greatest money laundry of all times. There are no objections from the communists who have even more funds at their disposal.

While some of the money from dubious sources remains in China, the rest eventually leaves in order to follow a circuitous journey to some sort of final destination. Usually along the way one or two, convenient tax havens are visited before the funds finally come to reside in a legitimate investment. Often this is high-quality real estate in choice locations such as Manhattan, central London, Vancouver or Florida's opulent coastline. In this way the value of real estate throughout the West, especially in the United States, has for years been inflated significantly.

This constant flow of money in and out of China continues to enhance the international status of the yuan. This bizarre spectacle could not exist without the underlying support provided by the US dollar. It is ironic that many international economists believe that one day the yuan could replace the dollar as the definitive means of international exchange. For obvious reasons this will never happen, and it's amazing that anyone would think so.

Subject at all times to intervention by the Chinese government, the yuan will always be the most manipulated of major currencies. Furthermore its current legitimacy rests to a large extent on artificial factors that obscure its inherent weakness. At any time China's national currency is never far away from a sudden and significant change in value. Eventually its fundamental instability will manifest itself in a dramatic way when the truth about China's economy can no longer be ignored – that all along it was nothing more than a hollow Ponzi scheme built on exploitation and stolen wealth. At that time the world will witness a major run on the yuan and all assets connected to it. Everyone will try to exit at the same time and find the door already closed. The artificial, global stimulus provided by China will reverse itself with a major shock reverberating throughout the world. The greatest Ponzi scheme of the ages will experience the fate that always was inevitable. The biggest losers will be the many investors who chose to believe otherwise, especially the Americans - both corporate and private.

5

In recent years operatives of the Chinese government have continually manipulated the world's financial system through a variety of inventive ways. For instance, foreign investors have been lured in droves to the mainland where they have bought into all kinds of schemes designed to mislead. This includes supposedly valid companies with phony accounting, all of which are controlled by the government. Another aspect of this ongoing campaign of economic deception is China's systematic acquisition of important assets around the world, especially corporate. Typically the large sums of money involved come from others so the funding costs the Chinese little or nothing.

In 2016 China's economy and its currency achieved the ultimate validation when the yuan was included in the IMF's "Special Drawing Rights" - the basket of leading currencies at the heart of world trade. As a result the-once lowly yuan has been placed on a near-equal footing with the US dollar, British Pound, Euro and Japanese Yen. It was a major coup for the communists. Such a significant step sent an unmistakable signal that China has arrived as a supposedly reliable participant in the international economic system. It is one of many examples of misplaced confidence that would produce unfortunate consequences, many of which are yet to be realized.

To take advantage of this enhanced, economic status, the strategists in Beijing drew up an ambitious shipping list of valuable assets around the world. No doubt, they never expected to get so many of them, although that's exactly what's happened. Until recently they encountered little opposition gaining control of almost anything they want. In this way decades of laborious research have been expropriated. Now priceless, corporate assets in the US, Europe and elsewhere are owned by operatives of the Chinese government and its power center - the People's Liberation Army. Often "straw men" carefully chosen by the government have played an important role facilitating the process. For the most part all of this has been accomplished through an elaborate Ponzi scheme constantly fine-tuned as circumstances have changed.

The much-heralded Belt and Road project is a vivid example. The nations involved borrow at exorbitant interest rates from China's state-owned banks for costly, overly ambitious projects. The result is that China's government ends up controlling or owning outright strategic facilities on foreign soil that to a large extent are occupied mostly by disguised, military personnel. In this and other ways a regime espousing rigid, Marxist principles has for decades skillfully manipulated the international, free enterprise system, along the way acquiring a pernicious influence over the entire global order.

To this day gullible outsiders keep buying into almost any scheme devised by the communists. The fact most economic statistics in China are manipulated and the game rigged doesn't seem to matter. Even all the overt waste, corruption and capital flight (money stolen by China's own citizens) hasn't slowed the process. Recently a prominent US think tank (Brookings) estimated that the size of the Chinese economy is overstated by at least 12%. This figure is probably low and in some respects by a considerable margin. In other words the alleged economic strength on which everything supposedly rests is also largely a fiction.

With the Great China Scam masquerading as an unqualified success, the once-lowly yuan has achieved a status never thought possible. If all else fails, even more money can be printed that is skillfully managed by the government's captive banking system. In this way the regime keeps its fragile economy afloat by lending even more to the fake, domestic companies it owns (mostly SOEs or state-owned enterprises). *As a result mountains of fictional debt continue to be amassed that the government owes itself and, of course, never intends to repay because it doesn't have to.* All of this illusory activity draws even more money into the country to perpetuate the process. In America and elsewhere many experts praise these events suggesting the communists have devised a superior system (so-called "Red Capitalism") that should be emulated in the West.

One of the most conspicuous results of the bizarre world of Chinese economics continues to be the acquisition of valuable global assets - prime real estate; strategic ports and transportation facilities; natural resources, and some of the most prominent corporations in the West. This is especially true of those involved in advanced technology that have been acquired at an astonishing rate.

Regardless of how the acquirer is formally identified, all acquisitions involving China are approved by the government and promote its interests. If necessary, various manipulative methods are employed to aid the process. In 2016 the U.S. President's Council of Advisors on Science and Technology issued a report that noted China's use of non-competitive methods to facilitate the takeover of American corporate assets. Among others, there is the practice of competing Chinese companies colluding to weaken a target company so it can be acquired more easily or driven out of business. This is possible because the Chinese companies are backed fully by their government and often function as a group. In this way they foster an environment in which it is extremely difficult for competing, foreign companies to survive no matter what they do. This is only one of many ways the international, free enterprise system has been perverted in order to give Chinese participants a decisive advantage. Nonetheless, no matter how abusive the situation, a significant share of the world's most valuable assets continues to be handed over at bargain basement prices. The Americans aren't the only ones whose companies have fallen under Chinese control. Important, corporate assets in Europe and elsewhere have also been acquired. If the sought-after, intellectual property can't be purchased (usually with borrowed funds) it is stolen by spies or hackers.

In 2017 the report issued by the Commission on the Theft of American Intellectual Property, nearly 90% of the counterfeit, intellectual property entering the US originates from China. This relentless process of "creative borrowing" goes back to the founding of the People's Republic of China in 1949. Since then there has never been a pause. The only change is the methods employed that have become increasingly sophisticated and bold. Over more than a half-century the much-praised Chinese economy has been built on what can only be described as organized thievery on an enormous scale.

The systematic process of acquiring American assets is carefully planned and long-term. A recent example involves the state-owned Aviation Industry Corporation of China (AVIC), that over the years has acquired many, important U.S. aerospace companies. In 2011 AVIC purchased Cirrus Aircraft enabling it to do research and acquire sensitive information at the prestigious Oak Ridge National Laboratory. AVIC is the parent company of Chengdu Aircraft Industry Group that has produced China's new, state of the art fighter, the J-20. This important addition to China's military arsenal is based on the blueprints of America's advanced F-35 fighter that were stolen by Chinese spies. Subsequently all of the acquired American companies contributed their invaluable expertise so the stolen design could be utilized effectively.

Another example can be found in the area of information and communication technology that is essential to a modern, high-tech economy. While China is still behind the US, key companies with relevant technology are being acquired at an alarming rate. For instance, in 2015, 26 significant acquisitions were made in this area. In the peak year of 2016 Chinese acquirers bought 250 billion $US worth of foreign assets ($81 billion during the first half). 75% of the acquiring entities were formally identified as Chinese "state-owned enterprises" (SOE) that the communist government overtly funds and controls. During the period from 2007 to 2016 total, global acquisitions escalated rapidly while the mix varied. Initially Chinese M&A activity focused largely on natural resource assets. Eventually the emphasis shifted to specialized technology with China becoming the dominant, worldwide acquirer in this vital sector. Many of the targeted companies possess some of the world's most sensitive technology, much of it with potential military applications.

Relevant, global totals are as follows: energy - $158B; real estate - $98B; chemicals - $58B; *utilities* - $50B; *logistics* - $45B; *internet/software* - 53B; *semiconductors* - $14B; telecom - $10B. (Source: China Deal Watch). Over the years the Chinese have taken over a wide variety of assets by utilizing so-called "independent" businessmen. Supposedly this approach makes certain acquisitions more palatable to outsiders. Normally they would be reluctant to sell directly to a government although that's what they're doing. Among various sectors, particular emphasis has often been placed on companies that deal with the

American public including lodging, entertainment and movie companies. Legendary Entertainment, maker of the popular "Jurassic Park," is now owned by allegedly independent Dalian Wanda. Currently this governmental operative also controls the world's largest theater chain that determines to a significant extent which movies are seen by viewers in many countries including America. Normally it is illegal in the United States to own both a movie studio and a theater chain. Apparently that long- established standard doesn't apply to China. It's not surprising that many Hollywood studios now work regularly with communist censors to determine if a particular movie is acceptable to them. If it isn't, the movie is usually changed to comply with their wishes. A recent law in China bans any film content considered harmful to the "interests" of the communist party and its "socialist values." This is the new standard to which US film makers must adhere if they wish to exhibit in China. With most films distributed globally, American film studios are often the world-wide facilitators of communist propaganda.

Usually Chinese buyouts are not made merely to acquire a particular company or asset. Instead the underlying objective is to facilitate dominance over an entire industry or economic sector. An example is physical commodities, especially those with a limited supply. For instance, this includes lithium, a mineral used in the production of specialized batteries that power various, modern devices such as smart phones and electric cars - in other words devices essential to the economic future. In mid-2018 Tianqi Lithium purchased Chile's Sociedad Quimica y Minera. In this way China has gained control of a major portion of the world's highly concentrated supply of this vital commodity.

The situation is even more perilous regarding "rare earth metals," a unique category of 17 compounds with indispensable, high-tech applications. These include cell phones, wind turbines, lasers, plasma televisions and many others including various military devices. In 2017 China produced about 90% of the world's rare earth metals. Thus it is the only source capable of producing substantial amounts of these key substances on an ongoing basis. While alternate supplies are available, they are limited. Bearing in mind that all Chinese companies are controlled directly or indirectly by the government, the implications are obvious. Rare earth metals are an indispensable component of the "smart weaponry" relied upon by America's military. Without a reliable source of these metals any protracted war effort by the US would not be possible. In other words through this and other economic means, the PLA has acquired what amounts to a potential veto over America's ability to defend itself for more than a limited period. Any belated effort to correct the situation will take at least a decade and perhaps more.

China's monopolistic appetite extends to virtually "all" natural resources of significance. As a result the country's overseas acquisitions have focused on such broad-based commodities as aluminum, iron ore, copper, gold, nickel, tin, chromium, platinum, graphite and others. Very little has been overlooked. In recent decades the US has become increasingly dependent on outside sources for many, critical commodities such as cobalt and manganese - both of which are sourced largely from unstable locales. As a result supply disruptions are always a possibility. For instance, most of the world's cobalt is mined in the Democratic Republic of Congo, where China continues to gain political influence. Manganese is essential to the production of steel – one of the most basic compounds in a modern economy. The bulk of world manganese production comes from South Africa, Gabon and China. Similar to rare earths, the US currently imports most of its electrolytic manganese from China. A key application of this important substance is lithium-ion batteries.

In essence, the supposedly dominant US economy is dependent to an alarming extent on foreign suppliers of essential commodities. This includes communist China - a hostile entity. As long ago as 1990 the US was dependent on foreign sources for more than half of the 40 critical materials essential to modern industry. Not surprising, throughout this period China has followed a long-range plan of dominating global mining sources, especially those where the US is vulnerable. This is especially apparent in resource rich, sub-Sahara Africa. This cleverly executed, long-term agenda is nothing less than an effort to "lock up" permanently the world's most valuable mining and energy supplies. Meanwhile America has attempted to foster an international order emphasizing cooperation and mutual dependence - a laudable aspiration that China has skillfully perverted to its advantage. It is apparent that in any reasonable timeframe the United States will be unable to break free of its dependence on unpredictable sources of critical materials, some of which are dominated by China and will be indispensable in time of war.

Over the years a variety of financial institutions and groups in the West have abetted China's global acquisition program - in this way earning significant sums of money. Few buyouts involving China would succeed unless facilitated by foreign businessmen, who encourage this activity. As a result a hostile entity has gained control of much that is essential to the global community, especially those countries committed to democracy.

The implications of this short-sighted process can be summed up in a name most people have never heard of - "Magnequench." Unfortunately Magnequench is only one of many takeover deals that over the years have undermined America's vital interests to a significant degree. It is also an example of why America's rare earth metals industry is largely non-existent. Originally Magnequench was a high-tech corporation located in Indianapolis that manufactured neodymium-iron-boron magnets. In fact, it had a near monopoly on the production of this important device. These tiny, specialized magnets are an indispensable component in the guidance systems of cruise missiles and various smart weaponry such as JDAM bombs - weapons that are a vital component of America's advanced military arsenal.

Magnequench was a subsidiary of General Motors and with funds provided by the Pentagon developed these ingenious magnets. Eventually the company was purchased by the Sextant Group, a buyout firm run by American investment personnel. What no one realized is that Sextant was acting on behalf of two, Chinese companies closely allied to their government -- San Huan New Materials and China National Nonferrous Metals Import and Export Corporation. Only months before this important takeover, San Huan was fined by the US international Trade Commission for espionage. In other words it was publicly cited as a hostile entity, and there was no secret of their work on behalf of a foreign power. Without the cover provided by Sexton and its well-connected personnel, it is unlikely the sale of Magnequench would have been approved by the Committee on Foreign Investments. To make the situation even worse, Magnequench's subsidiary, G.A. Powders, produced a substance from rare earth metals that is central to the magnets. Following the takeover, G.A. Powders' facilities were promptly removed from Idaho Falls and relocated to China along with Magnequench's highly secret computers. The valuable information they contained included a method that assists the enrichment of uranium for advanced nuclear warheads.

Through Sextant's invaluable assistance, the communist were handed technology that has greatly enhanced the capabilities of the long-range missiles currently pointed at American cities. Whether the people at Sextant were fully aware of what they were doing as well as the long-term consequences, probably no one will ever know. Nonetheless, it is reasonable to conclude that some sort of large, financial incentive was involved.

After the takeover, all of Magnequench's US facilities were eventually moved to China. In this way the United States lost its principal source of these invaluable magnets. In addition, it is one of many reasons that China currently enjoys a virtual monopoly on rare earth powders. Also it should be pointed out that the two, Chinese front companies that acquired Magnequench are controlled by in-laws of the late Chinese head of state, Deng Xiaoping. He is, of course, the person given credit for devising the Great China Scam. Deng would certainly be proud of this particular maneuver, which vindicated everything he believed about the Americans and their preoccupation with short-term profits.

Some wonder if anything can stop this process of self-inflicted defeat in which the business and financial communities of the West continue to participate. While

European and Japanese businessmen are also involved, the Americans have a particular attraction to this activity. Many of the people involved appear to be immune to any concern about the long-term consequences for their countries or themselves. Recently there is reason for some optimism as the current administration (Trump) has moved aggressively to slow and in some areas halt this self-defeating process. An example is semiconductors, a device indispensable in a modern, high technology economy. In spite of numerous acquisitions in this area, China is still behind the US.

The largest and most important American company in semiconductors is Qualcomm that does extensive work for the U.S. government and Defense Department. The loss of its independence would have a negative impact on national security that cannot be overstated. For a long time Broadcom, a Singapore based company, has been trying to acquire Qualcomm. These efforts resulted eventually in a hostile takeover bid for the enormous sum of $117 billion. Initially Broadcom was a subsidiary of Hewlett-Packard Co. that divested the company in 1990s. In 2015 it was acquired by the Singapore-based chipmaker Avago Technologies that subsequently assumed the Broadcom name, in this way altering its public image. It is generally believed that the current Broadcom has close ties to the Chinese government.

Although Qualcomm continued to reject Broadcom's overtures, the Singapore company persisted nonetheless. A recent strategic move involved relocating the company's headquarters to the United States so it would be viewed incorrectly as a domestic company and subject therefore to less stringent rules. A pending Congressional bill (Foreign Investment Risk Review Modernization Act of 2017) will prevent China's state-owned or controlled entities from employing such an improper maneuver. In the future this legislation will provide important assistance to the Committee On Foreign Investment in the United States, a relatively small group in the Treasury Department that reviews mergers and acquisitions involving foreigners.

Because of this pending legislation, Broadcom accelerated the effort to relocate its headquarters to the US mainland. Recognizing the significance of what is involved, officials at Broadcom and those working with them weren't giving up easily. However, the Trump administration intervened by executive order to block the Qualcomm acquisition. In addition, the order blocks <u>all,</u> large takeovers of US high tech firms (essentially those vital to national security) by foreign companies. This comprehensive order as well as the long overdue, congressional action will significantly address but not eliminate a problem largely ignored for so many years.

Meanwhile American and European financial institutions continue to assist China's ongoing effort to acquire important, global assets, especially those in the United States. Also the process continues of "willingly"

surrendering valuable technology in order to gain access to the supposedly limitless Chinese market. In spite of China's long history of double-dealing and overt theft, many businessmen still believe a profitable future will be derived from establishing a close relationship with the communists. To this day the many illusions of the Great China Scam retain their hypnotic quality for the international business community and probably will continue to do so to the bitter end.

6

Since the communist party came to power in China, the most populous country on earth has devoted itself to one, nationwide program above all others - unrelenting espionage focused on stealing global, intellectual property on an extraordinary scale. In essence, for more than a generation China has repeatedly demonstrated a willingness to employ any tactic no matter how devious or underhanded to further this goal. Gradually this relentless program has evolved into a form of stealth warfare focused principally on the United States. It can be referred to as the "first war" or prelude to a second, ultimate war - this first war making the second possible and even inevitable.

Each year an estimated 500 billion $US is drained out of the American economy by Chinese espionage and trickery. The overall sum is nearly doubled when related losses are considered. In support of this comprehensive effort, *every aspect of Chinese society is utilized*. This includes scientists, academicians, businessmen, military experts and others. No useful skill or discipline is excluded. The amount of planning and the thoroughness of the effort is remarkable. Always the objective is to subvert the economies of other countries while cleverly manipulating the perception of what is really happening.

This massive, ongoing theft of global technology is organized and run by the General Staff Department (GSD) of the Peoples Liberation Army - the nation's principal, war-fighting group. Therein are found China's top military minds. While focused primarily on the economic sphere, the ultimate focus of the program is always the needs of the PLA. Addressing the interests of the Chinese nation at large and its people are a distant second. In this and other ways the approaches of China and the US differ completely.

Several, subsidiary departments or power centers of the GSD are involved. The most important are the Third Department that handles cyber espionage (internet); the Second Department - human spies; and the Fourth Department - electronic warfare. While only estimates are available, the Third Department is staffed by approximately 300,000 highly trained experts skilled primarily in analyzing computer code. Of late, the group's principal objective is to steal valuable technology by employing the internet. It is considered an honor to be an active member of the Third Department, where the incentives are substantial. Based on what cyber trail can be identified, it is apparent that within the Chinese hacker population there are several, distinct groups, each with its own unique style. The most noteworthy is known as Unit 61398. Considerable, professional pride is derived from belonging to one of these groups and successfully penetrating the defenses created to thwart them. This large scale, hacking operation is ongoing 24 hours per day/seven days per week. As a result the cyber defenses of US government bureaus, the military, utilities and private corporations are challenged relentlessly around the clock. It is not surprising that so much sensitive information continues to be stolen and often in the most flagrant way.

The number of on-ground spies or human assets managed by the GSD's Second Department is difficult to estimate. The consensus is that upwards of 50,000 overseas spies are active on a regular basis with about half stationed in the United States. These are carefully screened professionals, some embedded in America and its culture for many years. They are distinct from other operatives who function in a more informal way such as Chinese graduate students at prominent universities. In addition, there are the spies obtained within the United States. Some of these recruited operatives are motivated by simple greed. For others it is some form of bizarre idealism that results in enormous harm to their fellow countrymen.

In addition, as many as 3,500 Chinese "front companies" are currently operating in the US. They are devoted exclusively to the theft of trade secrets and specialized equipment that can be reverse engineered. While appearing to be legitimate business organizations, they have been created for the sole purpose of penetrating as deeply as possible into the US economy. As a result they often form business and social relationships of a long-term nature with their American contacts. The actual number of these front companies understates the impact of their subversive presence.

At all times there is a close, working relationship

between operatives in the various groups managed by the General Staff Department. This is especially true of hackers and embedded spies, who interact on a regular basis. This includes sharing information along with hacker groups protecting embedded spies, especially those with a plausible identity acquired over many years. As a result hackers will often create spurious trails to distract attention. This synergy has greatly complicated the problem of detecting where a security breach has occurred. Such interaction indicates the extensive planning involved in China's massive, espionage program. America and its allies have nothing that comes even close.

While of late so much emphasis has been placed on Russian hacking activities and alleged interference in the political process, the espionage capabilities of the Russians are modest in comparison. In spite of what many in the journalist community want to believe, Russia's cyber espionage tends to be fragmented and at times somewhat amateurish in character. The persistent focus on Russia obscures the real problem while China's activities achieve a high degree of success, harming American interests on an ongoing basis.

The raw information gathered by this vast espionage network is only the beginning of a lengthy process that also involves so-called "transfer centers." These elaborate facilities began operating around 2000 and currently number more than 200. Their purpose is to analyze incoming data and also reverse engineer foreign products so they can be produced cheaply in

China. Later these products flood international markets putting many of the source companies out of business. At all times useful applications for the military take precedence. To maximize their effectiveness, the transfer centers are connected to China's top universities and research institutes. Foreign scientists recruited to work in these institutes often end up assisting the process. Usually the valuable, underlying technology requires little or no actual investment by the Chinese state.

For private US companies, who are the source of most stolen technology, the situation presents an ongoing dilemma. Often a large number of Chinese hackers will focus on a single company searching for vulnerabilities. When possible, an on-ground spy will become an employee who plants espionage devices in a variety of locations including conference rooms and research labs. A frequent tactic is bugging duplicating machines so a copy of <u>every page</u> passing through the machine is sent to a Chinese operative. While information is stolen systematically from within the company, various, unfair practices in the marketplace weaken it further.

Ultimately the target becomes vulnerable for acquisition, or it simply fails and goes out of business. *While trying to produce a useful product, the average US company with valuable technology must defend itself constantly against the enormous resources of a vast nation state devoted exclusively to theft.* Needless to say, it is an unequal contest with many domestic companies ending up the loser along with America at large.

About 80% of all intellectual property theft and 90% of cyber attacks directed at the US business community emanate from China. As noted, the basic, estimated cost to the American economy is upwards of 500 billion $US per year. *All of this is nothing less than a devious state actor employing deception to cleverly appropriate the creativity of other nations - the objective to surpass and ultimately destroy those other nations.* Unfortunately the sacrosanct character of so-called "globalization" has been a contributing factor.

Traditional focused espionage is only one aspect of China's broad-based effort to dominate the global economy. A variety of allegedly "friendly" methods are also employed. Among others, these include joint ventures or "partnerships" between US and Chinese companies; ongoing relationships between academicians; and research projects and conferences that are really just a cover for even more theft. Also America's best talent is lured constantly with generous incentives to work in China. At what is alleged to be research institutions their best ideas are quickly stolen. While on the surface some of this interaction might appear well-intentioned, the purpose is always the opposite. Americans have a great fondness for joint activities. Unfortunately the Chinese regime has devised an endless series of stratagems to exploit this laudable trait to the fullest.

Currently many of America's most prominent corporations operating in China sponsor programs to assist the development of domestic talent. Cisco is building 300 Networking Academies to train a minimum of 100,000 Chinese students. IBM has active partnerships with 60 Chinese universities, and Intel is working closely with schools across the country. Google China's University Relations Program is connected to at least 15 advanced technical schools. The objective of this generous sharing is to assist the Chinese government in its effort to create what amounts to a limitless pool of technical talent. In this way it will be possible to exploit more effectively the vast amounts of intellectual property stolen relentlessly from US sources.

One of the most damaging ways that proprietary technology continues to be lost is the onerous requirement that foreign companies seeking access to the Chinese market must share their technology with a mandatory Chinese "partner." The continued willingness of American companies to comply with this self-defeating requirement is hard to understand. Also many companies go even further, forming partnerships of various sorts that inadvertently cause the loss of even more intellectual property. Both Hewlett Packard and Advanced Micro Devices have formed research partnerships with Chinese counterparts, while IBM is currently transferring much of its mainframe banking technology to its so-called friends in China.

According to China's 2017 security law, all companies

doing business in China must pass a periodic "security review" of their systems. This means that government experts will be able to probe into them as deeply as necessary. Also a company's data must be stored in China and cannot be removed without government permission. Thus if any useful information is generated from a so-called joint venture, it can't be exported back to the US. Only information from America can go to China. Also all companies on Chinese soil with 50 employees must have a resident communist party representative or committee that monitors everything that's done.

Through the assistance of US high-tech firms, China has recently developed a super-fast microprocessor that enables computers to function at vastly superior speeds. On their own Chinese scientists never could have achieved such a breakthrough that makes possible more advanced internal surveillance. Also US firms have been sponsoring a cooperative effort known as OpenPOWER that is intended to facilitate technological innovation in China. A Chinese participant, Semptian Big Data Solutions of Shenzhen, recently produced what is known as the "Aegis" program. This advanced system enables Chinese security personnel to *locate and "link up" (define connections) between virtually everyone in the entire country.* This, of course, greatly increases the danger faced by dissidents, pacifists and anyone who opposes the government. Already they face an uncertain future. *The obvious and regrettable conclusion is that the voluntary, technical assistance provided by US firms has greatly facilitated the monstrous surveillance state that currently dominates in China. Over the years these firms have been drawn into a clever trap, and at this point it appears that they can never extricate themselves.*

Needless to say, all of this self-defeating activity also produces disastrous consequences for America's economy. One aspiring candidate to the US presidency has emphasized his naïve belief that America and China should function as true, business "partners." At the same time there appears to be no limit to the eagerness of US companies doing business in China to comply with any requirement no matter how onerous. What these businessmen don't realize is that their presence is only tolerated in order to expedite China's modernization. When that role is fulfilled, they will quickly discover they are welcome to only a limited extent and one day not at all.

Meanwhile the relentless cyber espionage directed at America continues unabated. Much of this activity goes beyond spying on the business community and is *focused to an increasing degree on vital infrastructure.* Recently it was discovered that the computers of the companies that control some, key satellites were compromised. Potentially the implanted malware enabled hackers to change the position of certain satellites so they wouldn't function correctly. Eventually the spread of such malware could result in the global GPS positioning system being impaired, affecting navigation systems including those of airplanes.

The electric grid is essential to the functioning of all modern societies. It underlies everything making possible what is considered a normal existence. All basic systems depend on the grid, including communications, the water supply, transportation, emergency response and numerous others, even the internet itself. For more than two decades *America's electric grid has been subject to massive, ongoing, cyber attack. There are estimates that about 100,000 attacks often occur per day.* Not surprising, on many occasions key systems have been penetrated. If the hackers involved wished to do so, major blackouts could have occurred. It can be reasonably assumed that hidden malware has been implanted that at any time can be activated. Almost always those responsible for such activity are the hackers of the PLA, who have demonstrated repeatedly that they possess a significant ability to compromise many of the key systems on which American society depends.

A recent addition to this insidious process of stealth aggression is the effort by Chinese companies, such as state-owned CRRC, to dominate US rail transport. The ultimate objective is to control the flow of vital freight while also spying on the US economy from within. For some time CRRC has been buying up companies and technology prominent in rail transport around the world. For instance, in Australia there were originally three, competing rail companies. Like all Chinese entities CRRC is backed by the state and doesn't have to make a profit. As a result it was able to buy one Australian rail company and put the other two out of business. Now Australia is totally dependent in this vital area on a hostile foreign power. A similar situation is developing in a number of other countries as well, including the US. On the basis of exceptionally low bids CRRC has already won important contracts for rail service in Boston, Chicago, Philadelphia and Los Angeles. This is the familiar strategy the Chinese have employed for so many years in order to acquire assets and dominate global industries.

The use of rail cars manufactured by Chinese companies is spreading rapidly. Modern rail cars contain a variety of electronic devices. This is especially true of Chinese rail cars that to a significant extent are designed as rolling spy machines fitted with high-tech sensors. As a result they have the ability to collect and transport vital data about the movement of goods as well as the status of rail terminals and freight yards. The US military depends heavily on the internal rail system. If this process continues, operatives of the PLA will soon be able to monitor and even control freight transport throughout the United States. This includes the movement of vital war materials - an invaluable capability for the spy masters of the PLA's General Staff Department and its embedded agents on the ground.

Of late it has become increasingly apparent that spyware is implanted in most of the electronic products manufactured in

China. There are only limited exceptions. A significant example is the <u>*motherboards in the computers and servers of major corporations, government agencies and the US military*</u>. One of the dominant companies in the field, Taiwan's "Supermicro," has upwards of a thousand major customers around the world including in the US. Some have compared Supermicro's influence to Microsoft and its dominant position in software. Unfortunately Supermicro's vast array of custom-designed motherboards are produced in Chinese factories where they pass through a supply chain with many stages. It has been determined that along the way a tiny, spy chip the size of a gain of rice was added to many of these boards.

An inconspicuous gray color, the chip resembles a typical signal coupler and hence for years eluded detection. Instead it provides a doorway directly into the computer's operating system so the flow of information can be manipulated. The exact position of this spy chip on the motherboard is essential so it functions in most effective way. Because the boards involved are custom-made, they vary considerably in design. Of necessity, the factories where the modification occurs must be staffed by skilled computer engineers. In other words these are no run of the mill assembly lines but instead highly sophisticated, well-planned operations intended to pervert the finished, high-tech product in a fundamental way.

Currently compromised motherboards are found in

such highly sensitive areas as the data centers of the US defense establishment, the navigation systems of American warships and even some key facilities of the CIA. In essence, this tiny, ingenious device *provides the spies of the PLA access to many of the most sensitive electronic systems indispensable to America's survival.*

Another, less profound example is drones. The Department of Homeland Security has determined that much of the data captured by the aerial drones used throughout the United States is transmitted back to China. This information provides a comprehensive visual record of virtually every aspect of American society. Included are police and military operations, manufacturing facilities and even many people's backyards. Once again the spy masters of the PLA have not overlooked any means to probe as deeply as possible into American society and perhaps one day control it completely.

Of late, China's relentless, spying activities are focused to a significant extent on perverting the emerging global 5G network - the next frontier in communications technology. This is being done through a number of entities such as giant Huawei Corporation, another prominent company fronting for the Chinese government. Huawei is literally built on the theft of the valuable technology belonging others. The brazenness of the process is remarkable. In this way Huawei has become the largest provider of telecom and internet equipment in the world. It employs about 180,000 employees in 170 countries and currently earns about one billion $US per year. It is a remarkable success story, although one derived almost entirely from devious behavior. Important is the ongoing, financial backing of the Chinese government. As a result Huawei consistently underbids competing companies and has put many of them out of business while using technology probably stolen from them. Huawei claims to be independent although it was founded by Ren Zhengfer, formerly a longtime member of the PLA. In that capacity his specialty was communications technology that can be employed for espionage. Furthermore his daughter Meng Wanzhou is the company's chief financial officer. Credible information indicates that Huawei's funding comes directly from China's National Security Commission. Furthermore it is a strict requirement of Chinese law that "nothing Chinese companies do can be independent of the state." That admonition certainly expresses the point in unmistakable terms.

The advent of a global 5G network will enable mobile communications to operate at a speed 20 times faster than the current 4G. It represents an advancement of vast scope that will impact all aspects of global society - both civilian and military. Huawei seeks to dominate this developing, international system in a variety of ways. Especially important is the firm's proprietary equipment that will enable all information flowing through the system to be accessed. Thus Chinese security personnel would possess the ability to monitor all aspects of global society, especially the activities of the US military. In addition, the personal information belonging to billions of people would be exposed on an ongoing basis.

There are two, signal frequencies involved: the spectrum below 6 Ghz ("sub-6") and the other 24 to 100 Ghz (high band or "mm Wave.") Through its Belt and Road project China is successfully promoting Huawei's role in sub-6. As a result many countries have already adopted this standard and are using Huawei equipment, giving China a significant advantage. Through Huawei and also state-dominated ZTE, China's security forces eventually will soon be able to control telecommunications over large, geographical areas such as entire continents. In addition, they could at will impede or potentially stop such communications.

As the new global 5G network rapidly takes shape, many countries have convinced themselves that Huawei's products priced so attractively are reliable and free from spy ware. Understandably the US government believes otherwise and for good reason. Recently Huawei is being sued for property theft by numerous competitors, although at this point the issue is somewhat academic. Such litigation can take years, and meanwhile Huawei grows even larger and more powerful. With the background of the founder and other individuals who run the company, it is difficult to understand why anyone would believe that Huawei is well-intentioned and free of government influence. Repeatedly over the years this disastrous mistake has been made in connection with front companies acting on behalf of the General Staff Department of the PLA. It appears that many in the global business and political communities will never accept such an obvious lesson. Fortunately the Trump administration recently blocked the use of Huawei equipment and also prevented domestic companies from supplying many, important components. America's allies are being urged to adopt a similar course.

Huawei's ambitions do not end with 5G. Evidence is mounting that the company is also trying to dominate the world's vast system of undersea, transmission cables. These 380 bundles of advanced fiber optic cables carry about 95% of global telecommunications and are the backbone of the system that enables the world community to interact effectively. Also each cable provides a direct route into the infrastructure of every country connected to it. In essence, this vast cable system is another tempting target the spy masters of the PLA are determined to control.

Huawei Marine Networks Co., based in Tianjin, China, is Huawei's majority owned subsidiary (51%). It was formed by a merger with the former British company, Global Marine, the company that installed the first, undersea cable in 1850. With the other 49% of the current company in play, it is likely that soon Huawei (and the PLA) will control the entire operation.

In total, Huawei Marine has done important work on 90 projects around the world and is attempting to become the dominant company in the field. Pursuant to the usual pattern, most competitors will soon be put out of business. While undersea cables are vulnerable to implanted devices, especially during installation, their principal vulnerability is at coastal landing sites where tainted network management equipment and software can be installed.

Currently Huawei Marine is working on an important 7500 mile cable linking Europe, Asia and Africa that it will control completely. A 3700 mile cable between the coasts of South America and Africa has been completed along with another linking its important military base in Djibouti with the one planned on the coast of Pakistan. What China is creating with these three projects is a private communications network between its important overseas bases and facilities that cannot be monitored by outsiders. In contrast, most of the cables used by other countries are compromised to one degree or another. In time of war this will provide an enormous, perhaps decisive, advantage to the Chinese military.

In essence, this comprehensive "Digital Silk Road" augments in the electronic realm the far-reaching Belt and Road project with its potential to dominate global transport by land and sea. The digital system will involve both terrestrial and satellite communications as well as undersea cables. Because global communication systems can be seeded with a variety of malware and spy devices, *it is not an exaggeration that in the not distant future the PLA could possess a virtual stranglehold on the ability of humanity to communicate effectively with itself.* Once again the extraordinary scope and megalomania of Chinese strategists is apparent. In overall impact this two-part global scheme would equal or exceed the level of control the Chinese government and its security forces are rapidly asserting over its own citizens.

Documents emanating from the PLA's General Services Department often refer to what is termed "*hybrid warfare.*" This refers to the wide spectrum of activities employed to weaken and disadvantage opposing nation states. The tactics involved include "financial" warfare, "trade" warfare, "resource" warfare, "psychological" warfare, "smuggling" warfare and even "*drug*" warfare. At present, all of these activities and more are being employed aggressively against the United States. Such pernicious behavior comes from a nation that for decades the United States has befriended in a variety of generous ways. Among others, these include welcoming large numbers of Chinese scientists and students into America's finest universities and research centers. In spite of incessant cheating, China continues to be afforded the valuable benefits of the international economic system including the World Trade Organization. Unfortunately the regime in Beijing continues to betray this misplaced trust in the most cynical ways. In fact, it is apparent the communists in

Beijing view American generosity as an invitation to inflict as much damage as possible.

This is especially true regarding the importation into the US of dangerous drugs that on an ongoing basis continue to undermine the country's social fabric. The large and growing numbers of domestic addicts is a very serious problem aggravated by the huge amounts of drugs being smuggled across the porous, southern border. Most of this supply is sourced directly from China and is provided to the cartels at bargain basement prices. The obvious objective is to encourage as much smuggling of these destructive drugs as possible. In addition, many Chinese pharmaceutical executives operating in the US have also facilitated the process.

This is especially true of "fentanyl," one of the most addictive and dangerous substances on earth. It is 100 times more powerful than morphine and 50 times heroin. Even a very small amount can be lethal. While providing an exceptional "high" that addicts find irresistible, fentanyl creates a situation that literally invites death as the addict tries to experience an even greater thrill. In recent years the numbers of domestic addicts dying from fentanyl has risen ten-fold. In 2017 there was an estimated 27,000 casualties with an even larger group having barely survived.

China is the sole source of this dangerous substance that continues to arrive in large quantities at the southern border that smugglers and illegal migrants currently penetrate with relative ease. In early 2019 the various, drug shipments that were seized included one with at least 50,000 fentanyl pills cleverly designed so they could be sold easily on the street. Each of the pills contained enough of the drug to cause a quick death. If this one shipment reached pushers in America, it could have produced many thousands of fatalities. In fact, if all of the fentanyl impounded at the border made its way into America's so-called "sanctuary cities" and other locales, the damage would be incalculable. Although the total number of potential deaths cannot be estimated accurately, a form of visible depopulation would have occurred in some highly vulnerable areas. This is especially true of impoverished, rural America where the addiction problem is currently out of control.

Another example of substance warfare is the large shipment of one million pounds of unrefrigerated pork that was apprehended at the Port of New York and New Jersey in early 2019. Currently in China there is an out of control epidemic of hemorrhagic, swine virus, an Ebola-like disease that is causing a huge shortage of this key staple of the Chinese diet. Nonetheless, at such a time this massive amount of pork arrived at a busy American port. Dispersed in 50 separate, shipping containers, the meat was *disguised* as something entirely different (ramen noodles) in order to avoid detection. To date US pig farms are completely free of the disease. Regarded as something benign, the shipment of so-called noodles was nearly released into the country's food chain. If undetected, this large amount of meat sourced from such a contagious environment could have triggered a variety of destructive results within the United States.

This and other insidious acts demonstrate vividly the willingness of Chinese operatives to employ any tactic that will undermine America's well-being. The emphasis on espionage alone was eclipsed long ago by other activities that are even more damaging. According to the latest available figures, the amount of fentanyl sourced from China that has been impounded at the border could potentially have killed 794 million people. At this point it is apparent that China's ruling elite will stop at nothing to further its program of relentless aggression directed principally at the United States - the alleged, long-term "friend" in commerce with which many of America's largest corporations work closely on a daily basis.

A POISONED REALM OF CORRUPTION AND BETRAYAL

7

Ultimately all "Ponzi" schemes must fail and typically in a ruinous way. For a while they flourish in a spectacular fashion, acquiring numerous adherents before becoming unmanageable. Finally the indispensable flow of new money slows or stops completely - a result that is inevitable along with the harm inflicted on all participants. Soon this universal fact will be demonstrated anew when the grandiose "Ponzi" China has perpetrated on the world for an entire generation comes to its unfortunate end. Along with environmental devastation and genocide, the demise of the parasitic, debt-fueled economy admired by so many in the West will be added to the list of far-reaching, negative consequences caused by the rise of communism in China.

The objective pursued by the country's leaders was never to create a modern, productive economy - one beneficial to its huge, deprived population. Always emphasis in the economic sphere has been placed on the relentless pursuit of industrial power and especially modernizing the regime's focal point - the People's Liberation Army. As a result the economy was designed as an ingenious *transfer mechanism* that systematically extracts wealth and technology from other nations, principally the despised United States. To maximize this objective, all economic activity (both external and internal) is carefully "managed" by the government, especially through its fully controlled financial system. In this way favored projects are promoted while the all-important image of perpetual growth is perpetuated. The falsity of the exercise is hidden behind phony statistics along with the *accumulation of massive debt upon debt that will never be repaid.* Since all money is loaned to entities the government owns outright or in some way controls, *all debt is owed by the government to itself.* Obviously it isn't concerned about whether any of this money will ever be collected. The important consideration is maintaining the façade of legitimacy so the international community commits even more money and technology to the rigged game. It was assumed by China's theorists that this clever ruse would perpetuate itself indefinitely, and for a surprisingly long time it almost did.

Because in China there is no economic accountability as the concept is normally used, such a perverse situation inevitably breeds corruption, theft and waste on a monumental scale. At the same time productive capital or wealth is squandered relentlessly. Of late, the fiction that is the Chinese economy is becoming increasingly transparent and unmanageable, leaving the regime trapped in the inevitable consequences of its own, overly ambitious schemes. Although China's economy is heading ultimately to collapse, the gullibility of the international community seems to have no limit. Many commentators still believe the overstated growth will continue with China ultimately displacing America as the dominant global power. Such optimistic projections appear regularly in the western media and not surprising are generally accepted by the public. They are even repeated by many in academia. That, of course, is the strategy - employing incentives along with propaganda to lull the global community into a false sense of security. There is an obvious parallel to how the Chinese people as a group are being maneuvered into a disastrous situation that will not be appreciated fully until it is too late.

All along what is considered superior planning (so-called "Red Capitalism") has been nothing more than parasitic gamesmanship fueled by intellectual property theft and out of control debt. Based on simple arithmetic, it is impossible for China to achieve the predicted, global status or even to continue much longer on the current course. In essence, *the country has entered an accelerating decline (both economic and environmental) that is feeding upon itself and eventually will produce negative consequences that few expect.* For decades the entire world has been drawn ever deeper into history's greatest Ponzi scheme, and when the truth finally reveals itself, the adverse reaction will be dramatic. No aspect of the international economy will escape the impact. Then widespread recrimination will commence along with a new and profitable cottage industry for the latest group of supposedly informed experts.

The "Great China Scam" worked flawlessly until the unexpected occurred, and the first cracks appeared in what seemed an impregnable façade. The unexpected event was the pervasive, global recession of 2008, which caused the flaw inherent in all Ponzi schemes to assert itself. Demand for the inexpensive goods produced in China's factories employing cheap labor dropped off significantly along with the invaluable inflow of new funds. In order to compensate for these adverse developments, a variety of inventive measures were employed, most of which involve some form of indebtedness.

Over the ensuing five-year period China's state-controlled banking system expanded by $15 trillion, an increase in excess of 150%. This addition was more than what was added to the combined balance sheets of the world's major central banks where liberal accommodation prevailed. Since then the expansion of credit to prop up the Chinese economy has continued with hardly a let-up. *Over the last, ten years the debt amassed in China constitutes more than half of all debt created throughout the entire world - a staggering sum for an economy estimated optimistically at around 15% of world GDP.* Furthermore one-third of all of the world's corporate, non-financial debt is owed now by Chinese companies - in other words those directly or indirectly controlled by the government. Thus the economy in China has only remained afloat on what amounts to an ongoing illusion.

During the first, two months of 2016, over $1 trillion of debt was added. Three years later the process continues. In January 2019, $685 billion of new money was injected into the banking system or about 5% of the nation's entire GDP. (In only one month that is more than the GDP of oil-rich Saudi Arabia.) This immediately produced around $460 billion of new loans. Year over year the aggregate figure for March 2019 represents an increase of 80%.

Currently upwards of 20% of China's entire GDP is required merely to service existing debt - in other words to prop up what has already been squandered. As a result a significant portion of new credit has no productive result but merely perpetuates the vicious circle. In some key areas (especially commodity related), half of new debt services prior debt. Typically most credit is granted to companies favored by the regime that are the least efficient. These are the SOE's (state-owned enterprises) that dominate major sectors of the Chinese economy.

Meanwhile enormous amounts of additional debt continue to be amassed in the opaque realms of "shadow banking" and various, non-official sectors impossible to monitor. This sum is estimated in excess of $10 trillion or more than the nation's entire GDP (realistically estimated). In addition, there is the massive debt issued by local governments through so-called Local Government Finance Vehicles (LGFV).

While these numbers are based on information generally available, most observers agree that all statistics in China must be viewed with skepticism. As a result it isn't possible to know with accuracy how much debt really exists in China. Fudging statistics has always been part of the game, and the communists have no incentive to do otherwise. This is especially true regarding the balance sheets of every, supposedly independent company operating in China. It is the reason that so many are heading toward insolvency or have already reached a terminal stage. For the regime whatever rationale existed for keeping them alive has vanished. As a result they will be left to fail with little concern for the consequences, especially for investors - foreign or domestic.

Regardless of whether the "official" numbers are believed or not, it is an inescapable fact that *China remains afloat on an enormous mountain of dubious, uncollectible credit that is growing inexorably larger*. In this way the regime continues to postpone the inevitable hoping the old days will return when limitless amounts of outside money were available on any pretext. For the communists it was a dream come true that is gone forever. Entry into the World Trade Organization and a massive real estate boom assisted the illusion of invincibility.

An important issue is the relationship of "reported" debt to alleged GDP or productive output. Once again questionable figures are involved. China's widely reported GDP is probably inflated by upwards of 20%. (A recent estimate by Brookings is 12%.) Furthermore most GDP numbers usually omit certain, key factors such as industrial-related, environmental damage (a form of depreciation). Also at various times a significant portion of the stated number involves questionable, make-work projects that produce little or no tangible return. Ultimately they become nothing more than another drag on the overall economy. This includes the construction of so-called "ghost cities" that to this day remain unoccupied. Bearing in mind that the $12 trillion figure is inflated in various ways, a more realistic estimate is probably around $10 trillion. Thus the ratio of overall debt to GDP is at least 400% or higher - that is, if one accepts conservative estimates of total indebtedness that obscure difficult to identify off-balance sheet items. This is nearly double the huge debt load of Japan considered the world leader in this regard. However, Japan's economy is highly efficient, while China is heavily dependent on exterior forces over which the government has limited control.

Various estimates have been made of total "bad" or uncollectible debts on the books of China's state-controlled banking system. These range from 2% to around 10%. However, the concept of a "bad debt" in China is totally spurious. If a company is considered important, the government will find a way to keep it alive. This includes providing the needed financing through a wide variety of state-controlled financial institutions. They number more than 4000 and also include city and rural banks and even credit unions. *Since the government owns all companies directly or indirectly along with the financial system, it is one giant, closed loop managed for the regime's convenience and the partisan objectives being pursued.*

It is not surprising that of late there is an escalating number of bond defaults in China, many involving significant companies. A few examples include state-owned Sichuan Coal Industry Group; Dalian Machine Tool Group; and Dandong Port Group that manages the important port on the border with North Korea. Also there are some well-known names such as the major, coal producer Wintime Energy and the highly regarded, financial giant China Minsheng Investment Group, which has $34 billion of debt. During 2018, there was a record number of onshore bond defaults with 45 companies defaulting on a total of 117 bonds ($16.3 billion). For the second half of the year, the number rose steadily. About 40% of yuan-denominated bond defaults were in the energy sector, which conveniently the government is downsizing. Six defaulting issuers are officially state-owned enterprises - in other words corporations for which the Chinese government is supposedly responsible. For many years it has been a long-held belief that the central government would always backstop any substantial obligation connected to it. In fact, this allegedly ironclad guarantee was often cited as a reason to invest with confidence in China. Obviously those days have come to an end. It can be expected that the pace of defaults in both the corporate and local government areas will escalate even further as the economy continues to slow. During early 2019 this is demonstrated by the fact that in only a four-month period defaults amounted to almost $6 billion or about 3.5 times the same period of 2018. In any reasonable economic sense this is a massive credit failure, especially since the anticipated trajectory is significantly higher.

It is not surprising that the banking system has begun the process of gradually imploding. Recently Baoshang Bank became insolvent and was seized by the government. It is generally believed that this is only the first of many similar events. No doubt, the government will resort to all sorts of dramatic actions in order to maintain the illusion there was ever a viable, independent banking system. This includes obscuring the extent to which the entire system has been a conduit for creating enormous amounts of fictional, non-collectible debt for political objectives.

Meanwhile rating agencies (also controlled by the government) continue to paint an optimistic picture, assigning about two-thirds of the nation's corporate bonds to the rarefied territory of AA+ or above. This total is even higher than the overly optimistic estimate during the previous year. No bonds in the entire country are rated in the so-called "junk" category. On that basis one might reasonably conclude that the Chinese economy is flourishing and there is virtually no credit risk - another of the numerous fictions that so many foreign investors continue to accept without question.

In China, a significant aspect of any default is a questionable balance sheet that includes alleged cash supposedly available to meet obligations. Typically this "cash on the books" turns out to be restricted or non-existent. For instance, in late 2018 Kangde Xin Composite Material Group reported 15 billion yuan of cash. However, only three months later the company defaulted on only one billion yuan of commercial paper. For Chinese companies such flagrant exaggeration is routine. In other words a phony, well-crafted image of alleged solvency is a key component of doing business in China. To the last moment this illusion is cleverly preserved with investors given little warning. Nonetheless, during 2018 the sale of Chinese bonds continued at a robust level with more than $100 billion sold *offshore* - in other words to the ever-gullible foreigners.

A key feature of China's unending reliance on debt has been the ability to "manage" the overall debt load so the process perpetuates itself indefinitely. In 1999 China first encountered bad debt problems on a significant scale. This occurred because the original pool of savings set aside by the industrious Chinese people (about one trillion $US) had been exhausted after being systematically looted by the ruling party. As a result so-called "bad banks" were created into which all of this worthless debt was dumped like oversize garbage pales. Thus the bad debt on the books of the country's four, major, highly respected banks was conveniently removed and replaced with freshly printed renminbi so even more could be lent to the nation's inefficient business sector. Some of the debt in the bad banks actually found buyers from outside, while most went nowhere. As far as can be determined, much of this debt remains in the bad banks while over the years additional, worthless debt has been piled upon it. Presumably everyone is supposed to forget that any of this debt ever existed. For the so-called corporate sector the often preferred approach is a "reorganization," which involves much of the debt ceasing to exist. The most incomprehensible aspect of this bizarre process is the way so much questionable or worthless debt continues to be sold to foreign investors of various sorts. This includes allegedly astute institutions. No matter how much money is misused, expropriated or stolen in China, the foreigners, especially the astute Americans, can always be counted on to keep the phony game going a little while longer. It is apparent they will never escape the grand illusion that unlimited profits await them in the vast China market - that is, if they only show enough patience and invest even more. It is a fantasy too appealing to let go of.

Meanwhile various, international organizations such as the World Trade Organization (WTO) continue to loan money to China at favorable rates. Also commercial paper issued overseas by various Chinese entities continues to increase. In this way a dangerous, failing regime is employing the short-term, international market as an important source of what amounts to working capital. Of course, there's also the huge amounts of hard currency derived from the endless trade deficit with America that continues to have a life all its own. Without these various, overly generous sources of funds, the dishonest transfer mechanism that is China's economy would have collapsed long ago.

As always there is widespread disagreement about the current status of the opaque, Chinese economy. An important aspect of this bizarre situation is the cat and mouse game involving communist bureaucrats cleverly obscuring the truth while the ever-diligent sleuths of West try to uncover the latest deception. It appears that both sides take a certain pleasure in this weird exercise, both proudly enjoying their moments of success. Of late (spring 2019), there is general agreement the Chinese economy has slowed significantly, although the ultimate result remains in question. During the recent, five-year period the rate of growth for imports and exports has been trending in a downward direction, and of late both are down significantly. The most likely possibility is that China has fallen into a recession that will continue for a significant period and perhaps never go away completely. Except for a small up-tick from December 2017 through January 2018, the rate of growth for the overall economy has declined steadily for six, straight quarters. During the last, two quarters of 2018, GDP actually shrank, an important fact China's apologists try to minimize. By any reasonable standard China is in a recession that is already impacting significant portions of the global community. This is apparent in the smaller countries of the Far East.

Since the 2008 recession the massive credit injected into the system resulted in the money supply growing about 10 times faster than in the US. Nonetheless to a significant extent this over-supply of liquidity produced only fleeting results and ultimately was transformed into even more worthless debt. Because all of this freshly printed money stuffed into the banking system wasn't enough to accomplish the needed objective, external borrowing has increased about $300 billion annually since 2017 straining China's finances even further. Furthermore much of this debt is short-term and denominated in dollars, which means it must be constantly renewed.

With almost all measures of internal, economic activity down significantly, the situation is aggravated by the unusual way the Chinese economy is structured. This includes over-capacity in the pervasive manufacturing sector created for the export market. An increasing amount of this capacity is no longer utilized as many, foreign firms move their operations to other countries with less expensive labor. As a result the related debt can no longer be serviced effectively. Also an inordinate amount of internal wealth is tied up in inflated real estate - the value of which will likely decrease. For the foreseeable future this will impact domestic demand because Chinese consumers have too much of their wealth tied up in this one area (75%).

This is not an accident but rather the result of deliberate governmental policy. The other, prominent area of internal investment is a volatile stock market afloat on huge margin debt. Ultimately both falling real estate and stocks will limit drastically the role of the Chinese consumer as a source of stimulus.

In sum, the overall picture of the Chinese economy is one that lacks balance, is burdened by massive debt, and has a limited ability to produce significant internal demand. Furthermore it is highly vulnerable to external factors that are becoming increasingly relevant to what is happening internally. At present the only effective remedy for China's strategists is printing even more money to generate additional, phony debt with defaults continuing at an increasingly high level. An immediate collapse of the overall economy is unlikely because the regime still has sufficient options to forestall the inevitable. The most promising is additional investment from outside. However, it is a virtual certainty that over time the pervasive, economic weakness will continue to feed upon itself and escalate to a crisis. For many years communist officials have demonstrated their remarkable skill distorting economic reality, and it can be expected that for a while at least they will continue doing so.

This unusual situation also demonstrates the complexity of modern economics where all national economies are interconnected in various ways - some to a high degree. To be successful at their devious game, China's strategists had to maintain a delicate balance between several, competing factors, especially those of a global character. It has been a difficult task although one they managed with considerable skill. *Now this balance is rapidly falling apart.* It was inevitable this would happen, although the elaborate Ponzi scheme perpetuated itself longer than anyone could have imagined.

For the regime a key focus of policy has always been the yuan and its level against the US dollar - the so-called "peg." This artificial relationship is so important because *it has enabled all exchanges between the two countries to be managed in a way that favors China.* As a result America has remained the primary source of the huge sums being expropriated from the global economy. At present the relationship between the yuan and the US dollar is probably the most important single factor impacting the global system. It is important to emphasize that the regime in China has always viewed economics as essentially political in nature with the appropriate policy decisions made in that context. Consequently the head of the Bank of China is often excluded from meetings of the Standing Committee when decisions relevant to the economic realm are formulated.

For many years, the flow of money into China was so strong it was necessary to "suppress" the yuan. If it strengthened too much the balance of trade with the US would have provided fewer dollars and hence a less favorable current account. This situation continued until the 2008 recession when it changed significantly for a variety of reasons. Among others, the vast amounts of credit propping up the economy caused capital flight. Also much larger amounts were borrowed from abroad. As a result it was necessary to "support" the yuan on an ongoing basis - a task that of late is becoming increasingly difficult. This is reflected in the fact China's all-important foreign exchange reserve has been shrinking dramatically and probably has fallen about one-third. Contrary to general belief, the selling of US government paper is not a form of retaliation but instead an unavoidable necessity.

At present the situation regarding the yuan is becoming increasingly strained with the available options in conflict. If the yuan is weakened too much to stimulate exports or offset tariffs, the cost of servicing overseas debt and other obligations denominated in dollars grows excessively. Also this stimulates capital flight (legitimate and otherwise) putting additional pressure on the yuan. For many years Chinese officials welcomed as much money as possible into the country. Now a significant portion of that money wants to go elsewhere.

Not surprising, in early 2018 the international Current Account for a time shifted to the negative - a situation that China's strategists moved quickly to correct by straining available resources. To make matters worse, the country's overall fiscal position remains fragile as the various sources of funds are pushed to the limit. Not surprising, foreign debt continues to escalate at an alarming rate, much of it short-term and in dollars.

What all of this means is the various options are competing, which undermines the delicate balance that was maintained for so many years. The skillful game has become too complicated even for China's astute strategists. Both time and international events are working against them with increasing force. As a result flight capital will continue to seep out of the country. This, of course, weakens the yuan further, encouraging foreign businesses to go elsewhere in order to preserve what's left of their investment. Hong Kong, China's window into the international financial system, continues to play its convenient role, which limits the government's ability to stem capital flight.

As previously noted, China's economy is not self-sufficient or even close. Viewed as an export powerhouse, it is subject to a number of restraints both internal and external. This includes the ongoing importation of large amounts of energy and food. For the foreseeable future the food issue will play an increasing role aggravating the country's policy dilemma. With the widespread outbreak of swine flu, the pork available for consumption could be reduced by as much as three-quarters - a shortfall that must be replaced. The outbreak of hog disease is a direct result of the diminished space available for agriculture. Massive pig herds are confined in increasingly smaller areas which breeds disease, making control of epidemics extremely difficult. In addition, the nation's corn growing areas are being attacked by a virulent infestation of army worms. The diminished supply of these vital staples along with the high cost of several, important commodities will add considerably to China's weakening international position.

The inevitable conclusion is that currently China is in a losing, economic position - both internal and external. For decades the country's leaders have viewed themselves as true masters of the international chessboard. They love complex strategies and mind games and have demonstrated their considerable skill in this regard. Now the game has become more complicated than they ever imagined. *The ability to control economic events is slipping rapidly from their grasp - something they never imagined could happen. Finally they will have to live with the consequences of the complicated game they designed with such forethought. Ultimately it is not a game they can win much longer.*

In China there lurks in the background one, ominous and ever-present factor the government cannot ignore. This is the possibility of widespread social unrest. In essence, restive Chinese society is never far from internal chaos. For decades the communists have exploited the nation's vulnerable masses in the worst way. In fact, the government is despised to an unprecedented degree. Their one claim to legitimacy is a supposedly flourishing economy and the prosperity it provides - at least to the modest-size, middle class. Now the specter looms that this all-important prosperity is slipping away. Knowing that they are not held in high regard, the communists are haunted by the prospect of a mass uprising and will do anything to confine unrest. This is one of the reasons Xi Jinping is employing such extraordinary methods to control everyone in the country.

In recent years the level of social unrest has only been suppressed by employing the most, extreme methods. The internal demonstrations and those classified as riots were estimated annually at 100,000. Typically some sort of layoffs or land expropriation was involved. As a result the average Chinese citizen tried occasionally to fight back, an act of futility that accomplished little. Nonetheless, the annual demonstrations briefly rose as high as 180,000 and perhaps more. Since then increasingly brutal methods of control have reduced the figure considerably. The regime knows only too well its survival depends on keeping the economy afloat and will do anything to achieve this objective. While appearing all-powerful, the government rests at all times on a profoundly weak foundation that could crumble quickly with catastrophic results.

As China sinks ever deeper into the inevitable consequences of excessive debt and mismanagement, the true nature of the clever scheme the communists have perpetrated on the global community is becoming increasingly apparent. Eventually the point will be reached when the truth cannot be ignored. The reaction will be harsh, especially among the many who have bought without reservation into the many illusions of the Great China Scam. This includes the shareholders of companies who squandered their future on the mesmerizing game played at the giant, rigged casino in the Far East. Finally the conclusion will be inescapable that the communists never intended to play by the rules or honor the endless obligations being incurred. To this day in China the age-old disdain of foreigners remains as strong as ever. Supposedly for too long those on the outside mercilessly exploited a weak and vulnerable China. Now it is only justice the favor is returned. This time the outsiders are the intended losers, especially the Americans, who will be left holding a very large bag stuffed with massive amounts of worthless paper.

For now what's important for the regime is to maintain the illusion of legitimacy a little while longer. Beyond that there won't be any reason to play the game. With the arrival of World War III, all "private" property in China will be expropriated and cease to exist. The foreigners were only allowed into the country to build up the economy. In return for their money and technology, they made lots of generous, short-term profits. This, of course, translated into higher stock prices on western markets. For a while everyone on both sides of the ocean was quite pleased with the arrangement, especially the corporate executives whose stock options increased substantially. Many were able to retire early and live in Florida next door to a condominium probably financed by Chinese flight capital. In fact, the new neighbor could be one of those clever bureaucrats or supposedly "independent" businessmen who helped the regime fleece the Americans. As a reward they made lots of money and then found a way to join the stealth exodus from their native land. Suddenly many of them no longer view themselves as Chinese.

Nothing forced those on either side to play the *great, economic game of the late 20th century*. It was strictly voluntary with China adding significantly to world-wide demand. Meanwhile the country's exploited workforce exported a benign form of deflation that globally inhibited rising prices during a period of massive stimulus through excess money printing. Economists keep wondering what happened to the much-anticipated inflation. The answer is more simple than anyone realized. Unfortunately most people in the West failed to understand that China was playing by its own set of rules in order to use the world's economic system to fund a vast and sinister scheme of extraordinary proportions.

The two neighbors in their Florida condos were participants in a drama more far-reaching and dangerous than either realized. Without so many like them, the rigged game never would have been successful or played out in such a fateful way. Both sides got what they wanted. This is especially true of the new friends in Florida with their shiny, new cars from Europe. Although once an ocean apart, they reside now in splendid comfort beside the placid, tropical sea. Occasionally on a balmy evening they join a friendly bridge game at the club house, oblivious to the fact that around the world momentous events have been set in motion that can only have a bad ending. For a brief time each of them played their minor but significant role that earned them those shiny new cars that look so impressive in the warm, Florida sun. Perhaps they will escape the ultimate consequences of what they eagerly participated in - perhaps not.

Now the great game in the distorted realm of modern, international economics moves toward its fateful conclusion. Eventually the once-benign deflation exported from China will intensify with the world economy following China into recession and perhaps worse. Currently the only global stimulus of consequence comes from the United States, and it's an open question how long that can last. Of course, there's always the trade deficit and even more money printing and debt to prolong the spectacle a little while longer.

The result of China joining the global, economic system was very different from what everyone thought. All along the communists were obsessed with building a massive war machine in order to realize the great, expansionist dream inherited from Mao. Soon the fateful hour will arrive to bring to fruition this most grandiose ambition of the ages that suddenly will engulf the entire world. Although exploited endlessly in the worst way by their government, the patriotic people of China will unite behind the communists who have treated them with such cruelty. With the state dominating every aspect of their lives, they have little choice in the matter.

All of this will happen and more because the world's economic system could be perverted so easily by greed and run of the mill ambition on a monumental scale. Also there is the all-important willingness to ignore lots of very unpleasant things happening in the plain view. These include the ongoing program of mining human bodies so the ruling elite and well-healed "organ tourists" can steal the precious health of the young and vulnerable - a monstrous crime perpetrated on a daily basis in China's state of the art hospitals. In addition, there are all those remote, ever-expanding slave labor camps that turn out vast amounts of inexpensive, consumer products for the convenience of global consumers. Of late, the orchestrated genocide directed at the Tibetans is being supplemented by the torment inflicted on millions of Uyghur Muslims. And don't forget all the re-education camps where increasingly large numbers of ordinary Chinese citizens are being confined indefinitely because they are guilty of some insignificant infraction that offended the sensibilities of a minor government bureaucrat. Now these loyal citizens are afforded the privilege of spending many hours each day singing the latest, patriotic songs while also experiencing the joy afforded by the profound insights of Xi Jinping "thought."

How easy and profitable it has been to engage in self-delusion about China's bizarre, new-age society and the rigged transfer mechanism that supported its remarkable

growth. <u>For a generation the global, economic community staked much of its well-being on a hollow spectacle it failed to understand</u>. It was a risky gamble, although one that for a while worked quite well. In the long run the result will be something very different.

8

Statistics alone cannot capture the scope of the environmental devastation throughout China. Because of the ruling elite's relentless pursuit of industrial growth, the country's vulnerable masses are being poisoned and their health carelessly destroyed. It is not an exaggeration that the residents of this vast country are living in a true, environmental hell that is getting rapidly worse. In fact, the destruction is so far-reaching it is undermining the climate of the entire planet. What is referred to as "global warming" (excessive carbon emissions in the atmosphere) emanates to a large extent from a source no one talks about - China.

In late 2018 an episode occurred that shocked even the most skeptical. Suddenly a massive sandstorm engulfed ten, entire regions of China extending from Xinjiang in the west all the way to Hebei and Heilongjiang in the east. This includes Beijing and Tianjin, cities with a combined population of nearly 40 million inhabitants. In the northwest a giant wall of sand particles *100 meters high moving at a speed of 17 meters per second* swept violently over the land suddenly engulfing many cities along the way like Zhangye and Golmud. For two days a major portion of China's enormous landmass was covered by a semi-dark, nicotine-colored smog of fine sand that severely damages human lungs. Ultimately the storm reached almost to showcase Shanghai. Several months before there was a prelude of things to come when tens of thousands of "smog refugees" fled the poisonous air in portions of northern China. What this latest storm demonstrates in unmistakable terms is that the environment in China is totally out of control. Eventually many locales will be uninhabitable. Some already fall into that category, although large numbers of people continue to live in such places.

Few outside China are aware how completely the country's environment has been ruined by overly rapid industrialization. It is the bitter price paid to fulfill the regime's ambitious goals. Not surprising, many Chinese citizens want to leave their country. This includes members of the ruling communist party, who realize that in many respects time is running out. Determined to slow and even halt the exodus, the government continues to tighten its iron grip. Eventually leaving China will no longer be possible even for those employing the riskiest strategies.

Meanwhile glamorous images of the showcase cities of the Gold Coast continue to appear regularly on American television. Supposedly hundreds of millions of ordinary people have been lifted compassionately out of poverty as capitalism along with a fledgling democracy takes hold - a cynical fiction that the western media continues to promote. In reality, the vast majority of Chinese citizens barely scrape out a pitiful existence amid the devastated environment, many dispossessed from their land because of the wasteful projects benefiting the politically powerful. The vast, bleak interior has been compared to something out of the stone age, where nearly a billion, uneducated "peasants" survive on an income of only a few dollars a day. Many have no discernable income. Not surprising, this remote area cut off from the rest of the world is the location of the infamous Laogai (Laodong Gaizao), the massive penal system where millions of forgotten souls are worked to death to produce cheap products for export. Now in isolated Xinjiang province, millions of Uyghur Muslims have been herded into concentration camps. There are reliable reports of systematic brainwashing, and it is reasonable to conclude that the groundwork is being laid for another, large-scale genocide. First the Falun Gong followed by the inhabitants of Tibet - now the Uyghurs. As history has demonstrated repeatedly, a government that relies on organized cruelty always seeks out new victims and finds them as it progresses relentlessly from one group to another.

While the regime continues to demonstrate its total indifference to humanitarian values, the environmental destruction in China continues to accelerate. Since 1949, the land suitable for living in China has shrunk from six million square kilometers to only three million - an area that is becoming increasingly polluted. Beijing, the country's capital, is estimated to have the second worst living environment among the world's 40 major cities. The population in many areas of China is riddled with the worst forms of cancer. A once-fertile area of grasslands double the size of Great Britain has been transformed into a vast, roaming desert that soon will threaten Beijing's survival. At times in various locales there are damaging, man-made earthquakes. After the reservoir behind the Zipingpu dam in Sichuan province was filled, a massive earthquake was triggered killing more than 70,000 people.

Pollution contaminates coastal areas and the nearby sea with many sewage outlets located near fish farms. The northeastern Bohai Sea, once known as the "Ocean Park" or "Fish Warehouse," was traditionally one of the richest fishing areas in the Far East. Now virtually all marine life has perished there. Each year 5.7 billion tons of toxic waste and 2 billion tons of solid waste are deposited in the Bohai. It is now so polluted a cleanup could take at least a century and probably more. The smog and acid rain emanating from China's factories impact forests as far away as Indonesia. Nothing conveys the environmental tragedy of modern-day China more than the insidious plague of rats that periodically erupts somewhere in the country. Near Dongting Lake, China's second largest, an estimated 2 billion rats suddenly invaded farming communities in 20 counties. They ravaged four million acres of farmland requiring the most determined efforts to keep them at bay.

All of this environmental ruin can be traced directly to over-industrialization and the government's misguided, environmental schemes that abet the ruin. Often local weather bureaus are forbidden to provide alerts, especially regarding the poisonous smog that blankets major population centers such as

Beijing. It is not surprising the regime views reports about adverse, environmental conditions as a threat to social order. There have even been attempts to equate such reporting with disclosing "national secrets."

One of the most significant aspects of this pervasive ruin is the *destruction of China's limited water resources*. Because of geography such resources have always been limited. With 20% of the world's population, China has less than seven percent of the water. Furthermore, there are significant regional imbalances with 80% of the water located in the south while much of the farming is in the north - the same area where industrial development causes so much pollution.

Currently more than half of the population has immediate access only to polluted drinking water. 90% of the country's invaluable groundwater is polluted, and half of China's 55,000 rivers have disappeared completely. 80% of those that remain are polluted. Some are so poisoned with industrial chemicals they cannot be touched while others can be set on fire with a match. There are more than 21,000 large chemical plants along the remaining waterways, most with little ability to clean discharged waste. About 60% of the country's once pristine lakes are unfit for human use.

The mighty, 3,964 mile long Yangtze, China's longest and most important river, is rapidly turning cancerous. Although it was considered too large to be poisoned, almost all maritime species in the river perished years ago. The government's official position is that the water is completely safe. The major cities along the Yangtze include Shanghai, Chongqing, Wuhan and Nanjing. Each year a total of more than 30,000,000,000 tons of industrial and human waste are deposited directly into the Yangtze, at least 80% untreated in any way. Of the 400 cities along the river, half use it as their primary source of drinking water. In recent years a long stretch of this enormous river suddenly turned a bright vermillion color from chemical pollution emitted from an unknown source.

The much-heralded Three Gorges Dam, one of China's most celebrated infrastructure projects, has been a major contributor to the rapid decline of the Yangtze. In spite of laudatory claims to the contrary, the dam is really another, overly ambitious scheme that has failed miserably. Four million people were displaced during construction and $25 billion expended to create the largest hydroelectric project in the world. In spite of official efforts to conceal the adverse effects, it is apparent that irreversible, long-term damage has been inflicted on the country's most important river. Along with the dam itself, the ongoing accumulation of sediment is slowing the water's flow. This includes the 400 mile-long reservoir behind the dam. As a result the river cannot cleanse itself effectively, abetting the contamination. Nonetheless, the project continues to be extolled globally as another great triumph of China's advanced, socialist planning.

One-third of China is now a vast and rapidly expanding desert. The continued growth of the country's deserts is occurring at a rate 18 times the world average. Sandstorms are 20 times more frequent than in the 1960s. A massive desert continues to spread eastward across the North China plain, where much of the country's wheat is grown. Once considered the world's largest and most beautiful alpine wetland, the Zoige wetland has shrunk more than 70% because of desertification. Two-thirds of the 300 pristine lakes in the area have disappeared completely. In addition, the Zoige is the fountainhead for the famed Yellow River that is drying up rapidly. At certain times of the year it hardly exists at all.

After the founding of the People's Republic of China, vast numbers of trees were felled indiscriminately causing valuable forests to shrink drastically. Recognizing the problem, a massive reforestation project commenced that planted 66 billion trees that supposedly would create 405 million hectares of new forest covering 42% of China's territory. With pride the project was named the "Great Green Wall" and heralded as another triumph of the country's progressive system. Unfortunately things didn't work out as expected. In order to expedite progress, fast-growing, non-native species were introduced while local buckhorn and others that stabilized the soil were carelessly uprooted. The non-native trees such as pine and popular require large amounts of water, which shrank the water table far below its original depth. At this level the root systems of the native grasses died off rapidly, causing even more desertification. Now a situation exists that cannot be reversed within any foreseeable timeframe and perhaps never.

Eventually the vast, roaming desert approaching Beijing could consume the entire city. Each year massive sand storms sweep over the city depositing more than 1,000,000 tons of dust and sand. Already large sand dunes are less than 70 kilometers away. At the current rate the desert could reach the outskirts of Beijing in less than 15 years - that is, unless the process accelerates, which is the likely scenario.

In spite of optimistic reports to the contrary, the government is not winning its war against desertification or any aspect of the pervasive, environmental degradation. A prestigious academy has concluded that at times Beijing is barely suitable for human habitation. At one point during 2015, the air in the city was polluted to a level 7200% above the acceptable level defined by the World Health Organization. In other words it was extremely harmful unless a person was wearing the type of breathing mask used in auto body paint booths. It's not surprising that reports regarding air quality in the city are often curtailed, which prevents the average citizen from taking any protective measures.

The Natural Science Foundation of China has reported extensive land settlement in over 50 major cities due to extracting excessively large amounts of water from underground aquifers. This priceless resource thousands of years old is almost completely exhausted and soon will be gone forever. The affected cities include scenic Shanghai where many of the city's impressive skyscrapers face an uncertain future. In large areas of Beijing the ground is sinking at an accelerating rate of four to five inches per year. This includes Chaoyang in the heart of the city where many important buildings are located. At the current rate some of these buildings along with infrastructure could eventually crumble into heaps of rubble. This would occur as a prelude to the arrival of the massive desert that continues to move inexorably toward the city.

The nation of China can no longer feed itself and must depend on foreign sources to sustain its population. 40% of the limited farmland is contaminated by arsenic and dangerous heavy metals - a profoundly harmful situation causing escalating rates of cancer and birth defects. Soil contamination of this sort cannot be easily reversed. In fact, it continues to get worse. Also what land is available for cultivation continues to shrink because of the endless, construction projects that inflate GDP numbers. For centuries much of China was dedicated to small-parcel, subsistence farming that fed large numbers of people. It was a very effective system emphasizing personal stewardship that evolved gradually over time. Nonetheless, each year upwards of one million, Chinese citizens lose their small parcel of land and only means of livelihood to forced expropriation by local governments and corrupt business interests.

China's invaluable North China Plain is sinking noticeably as excessive amounts of water continue to be extracted from deep underground. While the food situation worsens, even more territory is damaged. As a result a significant amount of the food produced in China comes from contaminated land, some of this food unfit for consumption. There are legitimate questions as to how much is exported abroad.

A vivid example of this situation is the seafood produced on giant fish farms. This industry has enabled China to become the largest seafood exporter in the world. Many farms are located in coastal areas heavily contaminated by mercury, lead and other metals. Some farms have moved inland to avoid this problem quickly contaminating local water supplies. Fish farming requires large amounts of water. For instance, at one facility dedicated to eel farming, 5,000 tons of seafood are produced per year. This requires 280 million gallons of water per day that is discharged back into the local supply. Whether seafood farming takes place on the coast or inland, there simply is not enough clean water to produce an uncontaminated product. The result is that many fish farmers employ veterinary drugs and pesticides so their fish remain healthy long enough to be harvested. The idea that such methods are not used is not plausible.

The most conspicuous result of this destructive situation is the ongoing damage inflicted on the health of the average Chinese citizen. At least half of the population suffers from environmental-related illnesses, and 225 million have significant mental disorders rooted in stress. Half of the population is estimated to be pre-diabetic. 85% of deaths in China are caused by non-communicable diseases such as respiratory and cardiovascular disease. It is estimated that in 20 years there will be more people suffering from age-related diseases such as Alzheimer's than all of the developed nations combined. What these statistics have in common is severe stress on the human body related to adverse living conditions. It is apparent the horror show that is the environment in China will only grow even worse. Meanwhile 80% of the nation's limited healthcare budget is spent on only 8.5 million top-ranking government officials.

One of the most tragic consequences of this situation is the rapid spread of birth defects in China, which leads the world in this regard. Of approximately 20 million babies born each year, an estimated 300,000 have serious birth defects. Thus every 30 seconds a baby with a significant defect is born in China. About a third of these babies die fairly soon. In other words they have been damaged so severely that even advanced medicine cannot save them. The correlation between environmental contamination and birth defects is well-documented. For instance, there is a particularly high incidence of such defects in Shanxi province, where much of the nation's sulfur-ridden coal is produced and burned.

In sum, *China is heading inevitably toward environmental collapse.* This relentless process will only intensify with the ultimate result unavoidable. In the meantime even more damage will be inflicted on the health of the average Chinese citizen, who has little to say about the matter. The changes necessary to avert such a tragedy are difficult to implement and take time. As a result they will not be implemented by a government preoccupied with grandiose schemes. Instead of being concerned about the well-being of the people, it is committed irrevocably to the messianic obsession of growing China's power in order to realize the country's presumed, historical destiny. Supposedly in this way the inequities of the past will be redressed, and the superior culture of the Han people finally recognized after so many years of foreign domination.

It is apparent that the willingness of China's leaders to tolerate such extraordinary damage to their own homeland always had an element of premeditation. At some point the decision was made to sacrifice traditional China for a grandiose purpose - to acquire the means to win a monumental war of conquest for new territory of vast proportions. This is the great, patriotic conflict envisaged long ago by Mao Zedong. With problems compounding themselves, China's obsessive leaders cannot wait much longer or risk being overtaken by the many, adverse developments they have caused. Soon they must act or risk being swept from power as the historical process they seek to dominate moves relentlessly ahead threatening to leave them defeated in its wake.

9

Each year large numbers of Chinese citizens find a way to leave their country - many having previously exported significant sums of money that were probably stolen or embezzled. This includes many members of the communist party. Knowing that unfortunate things lie ahead in China, most just want to go anywhere they can. Except for the country's ruling elite, little loyalty is left to the great, socialist experiment. Although everyone is being "watched" to an unpredicted degree, the government has been unable to halt the exodus completely. With the environment deteriorating rapidly and the level of social control continuing to escalate, "fear" is the primary force holding Chinese society together. In essence, it is the glue that prevents the collapse of a crumbling system rapidly being transformed into a true "Marxist-Leninist" prison of vast proportions. Eventually the stealth flight out of China will become even more desperate, although most will be forced to remain behind and live with the grotesque reality rapidly coming to fruition inside mainland China .

In recent years an estimated 1.5 million party members have been disciplined for various, perceived transgressions, many rounded up during mass arrests. Often there was no warning or legal procedures involved. Some served prison sentences while others were quietly executed. With the pervasive, surveillance system reaching now into every corner of the nation, the regime punishes even minor acts considered unconventional. The passports of provincial, governmental officials were confiscated because so many failed to return from trips abroad. Recently a variety of powerful commissions were established whose sole purpose is to supervise ("watch") <u>all</u> government employees, even members of the judiciary. Since most people work for state-controlled enterprises or financial institutions, this includes nearly everyone in China who has a significant job. It is the stated position of the government's all-powerful new leader that a more aggressive level of control must be asserted over <u>everyone</u> in the country. The stated reason is to prevent any deviation from official doctrine - what is referred to as "polluting" the nation's "political ecology." *Merely thinking in a contrary manner is considered "poisonous."* In view of the situation regarding China's environment devastated by over-industrialization and misguided governmental programs, such a reference to ecology is ironic indeed.

Across the country cameras and listening devices monitor behavior in the smallest detail, even where someone crosses the street. If the correct area isn't used, a significant demerit can result with the offending person identified and humiliated publicly. Thus the government's displeasure is invoked by even a trivial deviation from official standards. Contrary to popular belief, the Social Credit System is already active on a nationwide basis (early 2019) with many experiencing diminished circumstances. Throughout the country the re-education camps and "black jails" are growing larger to accommodate the escalating number of alleged offenders. It is inevitable this dystopian world will grow even more punitive and rapidly so. What lies ahead in China is "absolute" totalitarianism that will surpass the gloomiest predictions of what a government can inflict on its captive citizens. The perverse accomplishments of Stalin, Hitler or Pol Pot will pale in comparison. *The people of China are heading inevitably toward true "enslavement," and at this point there is little they can do about the matter.* Like the deteriorating environment, the social situation in China will only grow increasingly worse - and rapidly so.

Not long ago everything seemed completely different with Dong Xiaoping's historical thaw underway. At least it appeared that way with western businessmen suddenly welcomed in the country. Many were encouraged to live in China. The constitution was amended to allow freedom of religion along with the ownership of private property. Briefly optimism was everywhere. Unfortunately it was another of many, cynical "deceptions" cleverly perpetrated by the government, especially on its own citizens.

With the ambitious plan to build up the economy, nearly everyone in China was inspired to play their part and reap the rewards. The allure of getting rich seemed irresistible. This was especially true for anyone fortunate enough to join the all-powerful communist party. Being rich and prosperous was the dream that always eluded the average Chinese citizen. They could only marvel at the sophisticated lifestyles of the foreigners, especially the British and Americans. Now that was going to change, although the new plenty would be reserved almost exclusively for loyal party members and those who served the government. The unwritten policy has always been to lavish benefits on the limited group useful to the "cause." Even today grinding poverty still plagues most people in China - about one billion, so-called "peasants" mired down permanently in a pathetic, hand-to-mouth existence.

During the 1970s communist officials still lived quite modestly. As a result they rarely invited foreigners to their meager homes that usually consisted of a few sparsely furnished rooms with bare, concrete walls. Many didn't even have a private toilet. Now it's difficult to imagine that any of them once lived that way. At the time members of the party knew only too well how much their limited circumstances contrasted with the lives of visiting foreigners. The disparity was especially evident in the posh clubs left over from the old days of the imperial powers. While these symbols of the past are still admired, the envy and bitterness lingers on.

Nonetheless at the time most officials were grateful to have anything at all, even if it bordered on the pathetic. The history of China has always been chaotic at best. During Chairman Mao's "Great Leap Forward" in the late-1950s, an estimated 30 million starved to death. Ironically this occurred because of the forced collectives intended to feed the people. Like so many of the regime's grandiose plans, it produced the direct opposite of what was intended. Even today stories are still heard about the walking corpses with skeleton faces that were everywhere. Less than a decade later came an equally harsh episode in the unfolding of the grand, socialist dream - the "Cultural Revolution." It is a curious name considering the brutality involved. Suddenly the nation's youth indoctrinated by Mao's little, red book was empowered to terrorize everyone without exception. The supposed objective was a renewal of ideological purity. In essence, all were cut down to size and punished for so-called individuality and pride. This included government officials, academics, intellectuals and anyone who achieved even a small degree of success. Everyone feared being denounced, and countless numbers were forced into harsh prisons. Some of Mao's closest supporters suffered, even those who stayed with him during the most difficult times. Still the sacrosanct interests of the revolution transcended all.

Finally the great leader died, and the situation thawed. The prisons emptied, although many hadn't survived. They were soon forgotten. It wasn't the first time the nation endured a catastrophic event that would have crushed a less resilient people. With the party's precious ideology compromised, few believed like the old days when Mao was the anointed savior of a victimized people. In spite of prior excesses the party maintained its legitimacy as the only way to improve one's life.

The ruling clique that inherited power from Mao faced the difficult task of fulfilling his vision that already caused so much suffering. A key aspect was addressing the inequitable situation between China and the rest of the world. Although exploited for centuries by venal foreigners, the Chinese people, especially their leaders, always believed in the greatness of their heritage. The humiliations of the past were aggravated when the hated Japanese invaded during World War II. Hundreds of thousands were slaughtered, perhaps millions. Now the time had come for China to even the score and achieve its rightful preeminence in the family of nations. Always that was an essential component of Mao's compelling message.

The great leader understood that realizing such a grandiose aspiration was a formidable task. Overcoming the many obstacles fell to the crafty Deng Xiaoping. An ideologue like his predecessor, Deng was also a pragmatist with an uncanny ability to understand human nature and how it can be manipulated. With him there would be no self-defeating exercises in ideological purity - instead only carefully thought-out policies that furthered the nation's goal of becoming the dominant, global power. Thus emerged the ingenious plan to beat the foreigners at their own game. They would be invited into the country to claim the limitless profits they've always sought - the so-called "China Dream." At the same time their invaluable technology and capital would be expropriated and, if necessary, stolen. Before any of them realized what was happening, China would have gained the strength and know-how it needed. Outsiders have always underestimated what the Chinese people are capable of. Now that would prove to be a fatal mistake.

The scheme devised by Deng and his confidants was ambitious in the extreme. Most leaders wouldn't attempt something so complex. Too much could go wrong. But the Oriental mind is both subtle and resilient, something that most outsiders fail to understand. To people in the West, especially the Americans, the relevant timeframe is typically short, and they rarely look beyond immediate results. Exploiting this failing was central to Deng's scheme. As a result a sham economy would be created out of whole cloth that on the surface appeared to be western but in reality was controlled at all times by the communist government. In this way large amounts of foreign resources and know-how would be acquired while little was given in return. The exception was those short-term benefits the Americans can't resist.

Just as China had been systematically exploited, the favor would be returned. This was tricky business, although the scheme worked better than any of China's leaders could have imagined, even Deng himself. Success depended on the ability of party members and their associates to execute this ingenious ruse on which the country was staking its future. In the process some have become rich, perhaps even richer than many of the foreigners. Ultimately it became apparent that the average Chinese citizen would do almost anything to acquire wealth, even if it means betraying everything in which they once believed. Sadly enough, this includes destroying their own, once-beautiful country.

An additional problem was convincing the outside business community they're dealing with an aspiring 20th century economy. Of course, nothing could be further from the truth. This is one of the biggest deceptions of all along with obscuring the identity of those who currently control the country. As a result a supposedly independent business class was created that would "partner" with the outsiders. These favored individuals adopted the guise of western-style businessmen and even developed social ties with their new-found associates. The illusion was bolstered by lots of clever window-dressing such as young, Silicon-valley type entrepreneurs who supposedly work on their own independent of the government. Some were even brought to America for personal appearances like movie stars on a tour. Always the objective was to entice the gullible outsiders to play the elaborate game rigged against them. Many in the West still don't understand how thoroughly they've been "played," or perhaps they just don't want to accept such an unpleasant truth.

Even now China still doesn't have a real economy in any accepted sense of the term. A legitimate, modern economy has a productive focus that generates wealth and in that way improves the lives of its citizens. In China, the opposite is true with the government always the beneficiary. The fictional, private business community is still quite small and consists mostly of favored functionaries employed in such activities as real estate and export. Others are entrepreneurs who carve out a useful niche within the overall economy, bringing a degree of creativity to such a rigid system. Beneath the ruling class of the party and government officials, this sector of so-called, "private" businessmen is the other privileged class. Nonetheless, those who have prospered still represent only a small portion of the overall population. This serves the regime's interests because too many people, who consider themselves independent, would undermine authority. While this small, vibrant middle class has done well, they are never allowed to forget who holds the real power. Even the privileged in China walk a fine line and avoid politics. That's the compromise and to most an acceptable one - at least until recently when once again the situation changed significantly.

These days China's resident millionaires and even billionaires are often seen in the garish cities of the Gold Coast, enjoying the privileges of their precarious, new-found status. They have vindicated Deng's confidence that they would rise to the occasion and effectively play their assigned role. This is especially true of those chosen to "partner" with foreigners, who have willingly surrendered so much valuable technology that took decades to create. And so *excessive ambition in both*

East and West commingled. The communists found common ground with the capitalists, demonstrating anew the all-consuming role of money in the modern era.

While it appears the Chinese will have the last laugh, the country's newly prosperous have paid a heavy price. In a single generation the picturesque homeland that survived from time immemorial has been ruined completely - much of it forever. In exchange there are the 30 pieces of silver in the bank accounts of the favored. At the same time a stifling, totalitarian realm is rapidly taking shape in which no one is safe - Mao's crude dictatorship evolving rapidly into an Orwellian prison of vast proportions. In retrospect, the get-rich quick deal offered by Deng Xiaoping and his associates wasn't the great opportunity many thought. Now everyone must constantly prove themselves worthy of their privileges, even the top people. During Mao's era at least some could flee to the remote countryside. In current-day China there is nowhere to hide. The only protection is unquestioned loyalty to the party, and at times even that isn't enough. In place of the alluring prospect of becoming rich, only pervasive "fear" currently holds Chinese society together. At the same time the deteriorating environment continues to degrade the water, air, food and even medicines. Literally everything is tainted. *China is truly a poisoned land both physically and spiritually.* Even the drinking water in showcase Hong Kong and its lavish hotels is suspect. It is hard to believe that until recently environmental damage was considered a minor concern as long as production goals were met and more money siphoned into each person's private account.

Meanwhile large amounts of flight capital continue to exit the country often followed by those hoping for a new life abroad. Having grown prosperous helping the regime exploit their native land, many are eager to go elsewhere and forget what's left behind. The release of the notorious "Paradise Papers" provides some insight into the enormous sums communist officials have hidden in tax havens and other locations around the world. For years the most inventive techniques have been employed to circumvent currency guidelines. Even with the applicable controls tightened considerably, the State Administration of Foreign Exchange can barely deal with such a complex situation. It simply isn't possible to shut down the outflow completely. Every possible medium is being employed, especially the riskiest crypto-currencies ripe with fraud.

It is well-known that Chinese citizens played a significant role in the explosive rise of Bitcoin to $20,000 before a spectacular collapse occurred. Of late, the government is cracking down on the medium, although about 90% of Bitcoin trading continues in China. Recent regulations have caused large groups of miners to leave the country while many still remain. With communist officials unable to control the crypto-industry completely, it will remain an important route for flight capital exiting the country.

Triad gangs and the Japanese Yakuza regularly facilitate the clandestine movement of money out of China. Other convenient routes are the casinos of Macau along with the ubiquitous grey money changers of Hong Kong. One group in Shaoguan successfully "exported" more than three billion $US. Thousands of individuals were involved using 150 bank accounts with stolen identity cards. For brief periods "underground banks" come into existence for the purpose of transferring illicit funds. To date the largest scheme of its kind is a group in the city of Jinhua in central Zhejiang province that successfully processed foreign exchange transactions totaling 64 billion $US.

In mid-2016 about 60 billion US$ left per month with a peak of 95 billion US$ in December. During the entire year the total reached almost a trillion $US. Drastic methods were employed to dampen the flow. One problem is that the yuan is now an accepted international currency so it is converted more easily into the US dollar. Around the globe fake or altered trade documents are still the most widely used method of moving elicit funds from one country to another. From 2003 to 2009, an estimated 1.3 trillion $US left China through such forged or reused documents. The real figure is actually much higher. At times these documents also provide the means for fast-moving, "hot" money to enter China and then leave again.

With the outward flow continuing at a reduced level, it has become increasingly difficult for the people involved to follow their money. Using fake identities and other ruses, many still manage to get out. The objective is to live in one of the preferred countries of the West they helped the regime to fleece. In such a perverse situation the contradictions abound. The term "naked officials" is applied to government officials who send their family abroad while staying at home in order to amass even more wealth. The hope is that eventually they will find a way to join their loved ones along with their money. In mid-2017 the government issued an overseas travel ban that applies to government officials. A leaked report from the Central Commission for Discipline Inspection indicates that 77% of the delegates at the People's Consultative Conference and 58% at the important National People's Congress held foreign passports - something forbidden by Chinese law. Even top-level officials were involved. For instance, a former director of China's National Energy Administration (Liu Tienam) was found to possess 12 passports from various countries. The former chairman of the General Office of the Communist Party (Jihua Ling) had six passports and an additional six travel documents. A former vice president of the Supreme Court of China's Communist Party had six passports and three travel documents.

It is not merely government and party officials who want to leave. The situation is easier for so-called independent businessmen to cash out and go elsewhere. In 2013 an estimated 65% of high net worth, private individuals expressed a desire to live in another country. Already 33% had finalized plans to do so. Specifically, 60% of 960,000 with a net worth of 1.6 renminbi had emigrated or wanted to do so. This often involved incurring losses. The government has cleverly restricted the middle class to investments tied to wealth management products that typically underwrite favored projects. At times these investments are not easily liquidated. Thus what the government gave away with one hand it takes back with the other. Even with its own favored citizens the regime is always the big winner.

On an ongoing basis the large sums of departing money weaken the Chinese economy. Some of the funds belong to foreign businessmen and speculators, especially those who have been using China's banking system as an oversize money laundry. Now at times total flight capital rises to a level that threatens the entire system. This includes the government's all-important ability to "manage" the level of the yuan in order to perpetuate the oversize, trade deficit with America. If that isn't possible, the country's invaluable foreign currency reserve (at one time in excess of 3 trillion US$) would quickly evaporate with disastrous results.

Meanwhile the great Ponzi scheme built on limitless debt and continued exploitation of the international economic system is coming to an end. The exodus of people continues with a significant number still finding a way of joining their tidy nest egg hidden abroad under a bizarre name no one can trace. With social controls tightening even more, additional people are being moved to the periphery or eliminated entirely. It is hardly surprising that so many want to get out. Soon the draconian Social Credit system will govern every aspect of life in China. Thus the privileged middle class will no longer be so favored. They've been working long enough with the central government not to realize what's coming next. Already freedom of religion is forbidden once again. The feared Discipline Inspection Commission and the Bureau of Internal Security scrutinize party members more harshly than ever before, all of whom were recently "audited." It is imperative that the regime knows who can be counted on, especially when a crisis arises. Even repeating a harmful "rumor" is noted, which means any statement critical of the government. An official can even be held responsible if one of their subordinates commits such an offense. Potentially this includes an ill-advised comment at a social gathering overheard by one of the countless informers who these days are everywhere.

A new, all-powerful commission literally supervises everyone. Known as the National Supervision Commission, this secretive body exceeds in power the nation's Supreme Court and even the prosecutor's office. In essence, it is the counterpart of the Discipline Inspection Commission that monitors members of the party. *Thus more supervision upon* _supervision._ Xi Jinping's fanatical government is more determined than ever to root out and punish even the smallest act considered a transgression. Soon only a reduced core will be left in control of China, who don't care how much freedoms are limited. These are the true zealots, who in any totalitarian state always rise to the top and assume absolute control. At this point the regime's pervasive paranoia can only intensify.

Eventually the social control will be so rigid it will be impossible to lead a decent life on any terms. Then the world will witness the regime's catastrophic end game - the result of decades of careful planning and sacrifice which includes ruining the once-beautiful environment of ancient China. At that point there will be a run on the currency (yuan) that nobody can stop, and it will be too late for anyone to get out of China. Those who hoped to escape will be forced to live with the nightmarish realm their country has become - that many assisted in their own way in order to become rich.

With so many trapped behind the iron walls of the hardening, Orwellian prison, there will be no one to claim ownership of most of the money hidden abroad. Over the years it was amassed through so much betrayal and sacrifice but in the end will go for nothing. Probably someone will try to claim these enormous sums stolen from a sad country victimized by fanatical leaders obsessed with grandiose schemes rooted in the distant past. Thus an entirely new, international con game built on shadowy wealth will come into existence - the ironic fruit of the grand spectacle of deception and cruelty that is modern-day China. It is one in which opportunists and the naïve from both East and West have willingly participated. In the end it will produce only tragedy, especially for China's exploited masses who over the centuries had little to say about their failed destiny. Now they will be victimized once again while forced to endure the harsh reality of living in the ultimate Marxist-Leninist state along with the misery this perverse philosophy of the modern era always creates. This time it will also include a terrible and inhumane war of vast proportions.

WORLD WAR III - PREPARATION AND STRATEGY

10

At the 18th National Congress of the Communist Party in 2012, Xi Jinping became China's exalted, new leader and immediately set about making himself the country's most important, political figure since Mao Zedong. Currently Xi yields more unchecked power than the legendary demigod himself. According to some, he is the most powerful man on the entire planet including the US president. At times one might conclude that this vast country is driven solely by the will of one, opaque and obsessive man. In fact, Xi Jinping is not what he appears to be. Instead his rapid ascendancy that consolidates all power at the very top obscures the identity of those who currently control China along with the sinister objectives they are determined to pursue.

Prior to Xi achieving the highest post, there were some in party circles with broader support. As a result many favored a more dynamic figure for the coveted prize. With only modest achievements, Xi Jinping had one, distinguishing characteristic - a lifetime of uncompromising devotion to absolute rule in China. Over the years he had proved himself to be the ultimate party functionary, who can always be counted on to uphold the interests of the state regardless of the methods employed or the consequences.

In person he projects an almost comic banality as if two, completely different people are involved. In appearance he has been compared to the fictional, childhood character "Winnie the Pooh" - a reference that understandably offends China's ever-diligent censors. As a result questions linger about how someone like him could have risen quickly to such prominence. Also there has been virtually no opposition throughout the country to the extraordinary amount of power he has amassed. Suddenly he is referred to in reverential tones as the "core leader" and "helmsman of the people." According to the *People's Daily*, Xi is the new "*lingxiu*" supported by the whole Party and "loved by the people." Not since the days of Mao Zedong has the term *lingxiu* been used. For many the situation makes little sense, and that's because it doesn't. Obviously something else is involved.

Initially Xi assumed three, official roles: Chairman of the People's Republic of China (head of state); Head of the Central Military Commission; and General Secretary of the Communist Party (generally considered the most important). In addition, a fourth title was added when he took *direct* operational command of the nation's vast military - a highly unusual role for a civilian leader with hardly any military experience. In fact, he may have none at all. Also the internal security force known as the People's Armed Police has been placed under the control of the Central Military Commission headed by Xi. Thus he personally controls not only the entire governmental apparatus but also all means of coercive force inside and outside China. It is an astonishing amount of unchecked power in the hands of only one person. And all of this happened in only a couple of years.

In addition, Xi has established several, important, review commissions that he also heads. The objective of these groups is to evaluate on an ongoing basis every area of Chinese society, including the all-important economy. At the same time his grip has tightened on the party's power center - the 25 member Politburo that elects the exalted Standing Committee. His mandatory list of ten, "behavioral" requirements dictates what is acceptable conduct for all officials including those at the top. Of significance is the requirement of unquestioned obedience to the party, which is synonymous now with Xi himself. Finally he has also taken direct control of the vast, communication machinery, which has often been a problem for the country's leaders. As a result various, related groups have been reigned in including the Central Leading Group for Propaganda and Ideology; the Central Propaganda Department; and the Central Guidance Commission on Building a *Spiritual Civilization* (its actual name).

Furthermore Xi Jinping is also responsible for three, transformative pieces of legislation that focus on national security, anti-terrorism and foreign, non-profit groups operating in China. The most important is the unprecedented, national security law that outlaws anything that can be viewed as a "threat" to the government, society or the economy. This includes the realms of cyber and even outer space. *A so-called threat to the government is defined so broadly it has virtually no limit. For example, it includes both "opinion" as well as a specific "activity," which means that merely entertaining a negative thought about the regime is a punishable offense.* Thus the government has an unlimited ability to prosecute anyone who merely <u>appears to think incorrectly</u>. The implications for all electronic communications, especially the internet, are particularly ominous. Primary authority to enforce this unlimited mandate appears to rest with the new National Security Commission of the Communist Party that Xi also heads.

The second piece of legislation concerns antiterrorism and conveys equally broad powers to the government, especially regarding the high-technology sectors. Foreign multinationals operating in China must at all times be "secure and controllable." As a result such companies are required to provide their invaluable source codes so they can be monitored constantly for compliance. This, of course, represents a grave threat to the customers of these companies and also the national security of the United States. Nonetheless one prominent, US corporation has already complied with this extraordinary request. Never let be said that corporate America doesn't always go the extra mile to comply with the communists' most extreme demands.

Xi also assumed the improbable role of China's new "spiritual leader" - his allegedly profound ideas ("Xi Jinping thought") becoming the definitive guide for correct behavior for everyone in modern-day China. As a result his "Thoughts on Socialism with Chinese Characteristics" is regarded as a contribution of historical significance that has ushered in an entirely new era. These simplistic platitudes have even been honored by recognition in the country's constitution. This revered document already refers to Mao Zedong Thought and Deng Xiaoping Theory. Now a third pillar has been added. In addition, Xi' s ten behaviors - "Five Musts and Five Must Nots" - are mandatory for members of both the Politburo and the Politburo Standing Committee. Even the top people must constantly second-guess their behavior to make sure it conforms to the wishes of the country's new, all-powerful leader. Across the country educational institutions have rushed to promote the study of "Xi Thought" with at least 50 new university courses dedicated to this supposedly important subject. Also three study centers have been established in Hebei and Yunnan provinces that are dedicated to examining every detail of the great man's exemplary life and work.

All of this hearkens back to Chairman Mao and his Little Red Book of quotations that at the time was considered the ultimate, spiritual guide. Now China has a new source of inspiration. Instead of a handy book carried in one's pocket, a phone app is available so at all times Xi's thoughts are available for a quick, inspirational download. This huge data file includes his long and boring speeches (one of his specialties) as well as assorted quotations easy to recall. There is also admiring commentary by recognized, Marxist theorists on the president's inspirational life-quest to greatness.

Not surprising, a personal mythology has been constructed around Xi that has the character of a "creation myth." Particular emphasis is placed on his early years when he returned to his peasant roots, lived for a time in a "cave," was fortunate to join the Communist youth league, and ultimately overcome <u>all</u> adversity by his exemplary determination. Essential in this regard is his unwavering devotion to strict, socialist principles. One of his quotes that is cited often: "I am forever the son of the yellow earth." Because all of this is supposedly so moving, it is mandatory now that Xi's profound thoughts are read aloud at weddings. No doubt, this will enable the couple involved to enjoy a rewarding journey through life and achieve perfection in China's grand, new society of pervasive control.

In view of Xi's status as a virtual "god," many observers continue to seek an explanation for his rapid ascent to such absolute power. This is especially true because there continues to be virtually no opposition within the party or the country at large. Meanwhile the ongoing, disciplinary campaign he sponsors continues to intensify. The familiar word "corruption" is once again in vogue, which is the convenient term applied to any behavior not acceptable to government. At times there is even a growing sense of a traditional "purge" in the air with few in the party ranks not fearing for their future.

It might be concluded that suddenly the personification of mythical "Big Brother" has taken singular possession of this enormous country. *The truth is that Xi Jinping is not all-powerful or even independent in any true sense of the term. In fact, he is nothing more than the carefully chosen surrogate or "front man" for the those who really control China.* Without support that no one wants to oppose, Xi never could have acquired the top post and rapidly amassed such enormous power. As previously noted, what Xi does have in abundance is the ability to take orders and execute them to the letter. Ironically it is this underrated characteristic that won him the top job and his place on the global stage.

By remaining in the background, the shadowy group that controls Xi and through him the entire country is able to conceal both their identity and objectives. In Xi Jinping, his backers have been able to coordinate all power while arousing little concern in the international community. With global events evolving rapidly, it would not serve their interests to be known for whom they really are. That would undermine everything they are trying to accomplish. As a result it is essential the world accepts the fiction of Xi's improbable tenure. Among the many illusions about China, this is one of the most ingenious - and important.

To understand such a bizarre situation, it is necessary to look back at the late 1980s and the seminal event known in China as the "Fourth of June Incident." In the outside world it is referred to more graphically as the "Tiananmen Square Massacre." At that time in central Beijing more than 10,000 average, Chinese civilians were systematically murdered and at least 40,000 injured by heavily armed, combat troops. A large portion of the casualties were students from nearby universities. The corpses of those who had fallen were removed almost immediately to prevent an accurate count of the dead. According to government sources, only a few hundred supposedly perished and many were soldiers trying to defend themselves.

This blatant massacre was the climactic episode in a process going back years and was related to the loosening of controls related to economic liberalization. This fostered a sense of freedom that fed upon itself, especially among the nation's educated youth. In the mid-1980s the process accelerated on university campuses. The taste of even a limited amount of freedom was contagious and gradually spread around the country. At the same time significant differences developed within the party's leadership. On the one hand there were the reformers focused around Hu Yaobang, who encouraged even more liberalization. In contrast, party conservatives led by Chen Yun believed the situation was already out of control and advocated an immediate return to strict discipline.

This broad chasm extended throughout the party ranks. Eventually General Secretary Hu was denounced by the conservatives, who quickly gained the upper hand. In January 1987 Hu was forced to resign while a broad campaign was instituted that opposed western ideas in general. Hu died suddenly in April 1989, and there were widespread rumors that his death was deliberate. This inflamed sentiment even further. Student discontent increased on many campuses, including at influential Peking University. Also regular demonstrations began in Tiananmen Square, the nation's symbolic heart. This included a large gathering during Hu's state funeral that took place on April 21 and was attended by at least 100,000 students and their supporters. At this point it was already apparent that a permanent impasse had developed within Chinese society. The stage had been set for a confrontation that inevitably would turn violent.

The ideological division was especially apparent in the Politburo Standing Committee (PSC), the nation's center of power. On the one hand General Secretary Zhao Ziyang supported dialogue with the students while Premier Li Peng advocated martial law and if necessary the use of military force. Eventually Li was supported by Deng Xiaoping, the country's supreme leader, and a communiqué issued in *The People's Daily* referring to the demonstrations as a revolt. Nonetheless, Zhao continued to seek a compromise, even allowing the press to report the students' activities in an objective manner. On May 1, Zhao Ziyang and Li Peng clashed openly at a meeting of the Standing Committee. On May 13, a widely publicized hunger strike by students began, and more than one million people from all walks of life demonstrated in central Beijing. On May 17 a formal declaration of martial law was drafted at Zhongnanhai, the party headquarters. Deng made clear that he regretted the appointment of liberals like Zhao Ziyang and Hu Yaobang, no longer considering them capable of governing the country.

As these ominous events moved toward their inevitable conclusion, demonstrations spread across the country eventually taking place in 400 cities. The people of China sensed a chance for freedom and were determined to seize it. That was easier said than done. In Shanghai, Jiang Zemin, the municipal party secretary, responded quickly by sending in the police to round up and perhaps murder any officials who supported the students. His prompt action was praised in Beijing, immediately raising his stature among party hardliners.

On May 20 martial law was formally declared, and 30 divisions of soldiers mobilized in seven, military regions. Eventually as many as a quarter million troops were sent to the capital. Initially the army's movement into the city was blocked by large groups of civilian demonstrators, who risked their lives to confront the troops. Briefly the soldiers were withdrawn only delaying the inevitable. The demonstrations in Tiananmen Square continued and soon included large numbers of ordinary workers.

On June 1 Li Peng circulated a report that referred to

the protesters as counter revolutionaries while advocating the prompt clearing of the Square. In another report issued by the Ministry of State Security, it was claimed that so-called "bourgeois liberalism" had arrived in China representing a direct threat to public order. With this theoretical justification in place, the stage was set for military action. On June 3 three, hard line PSC members, Li Peng, Qiao Shi and Yao Yilin, along with the Beijing Party Secretary and others met with military leaders to finalize a plan to clear the Square.

The following evening a confrontation with the 38th Army commenced on Chan'an Avenue, and the first civilian casualties occurred. The violence escalated rapidly with large numbers shot at point-blank range. The soldiers even fired at nearby apartment buildings killing many bystanders. The demonstrators continued to resist, erecting crude barricades constructed with anything that was available. Soon more army units became involved throughout the city including the 15th Airborne Corps. This elaborate operation demonstrated considerable planning. Even armored personnel carriers, tanks and helicopters were used against unarmed civilians. As the casualties mounted, the situation took on a nightmarish character with the many casualties littering the streets illuminated by the flames of burning tires. Early in the morning the troops moved into the Square and rapid gunfire erupted. All lights were turned off, and in the dim twilight thousands were gunned down. It was a true massacre that took place at a location revered by the people of China. Later there were repeated attempts by demonstrators to reenter the Square, all of which failed. Under the circumstances their persistence was remarkable. Meanwhile sympathetic protests erupted in more than 80 major cities across China. A deep-seated hope for freedom had manifested itself along with an obvious disdain for the ruling, communist government.

On June 9 Deng Xiaoping delivered a speech praising the People's Liberation Army for its decisive action. He emphasized that the rebellion to overthrow the party had failed along with the effort to corrupt the country with western-style ideology. Subsequently there were mass arrests with many executed, some having only a tenuous relationship to the uprising. An unmistakable object lesson was being sent to the country at large, and in explicit terms everyone was being warned to avoid similar activity in the future. Otherwise the government would employ as much raw coercion as necessary. It was apparent the party had been altered completely with many of its members no longer willing to accept the hollow rhetoric about enlightened "socialism."

As a result the party's leadership promptly changed. Zhao Ziyang was expelled from the Standing Committee, and Wan Li, who also opposed military action, placed under arrest. Praised for his cruel and decisive response in Shanghai, Jiang Zemin was elevated to General Secretary of the Communist Party. This troubling episode made possible the poisonous role he continues to play in Chinese history. Recognizing Tiananmen Square as an opportunity, he moved immediately to take full advantage of it and institute the use of the blatant cruelty that is his hallmark.

A systematic purge of the party rank and file commenced that lasted a year and a half - anyone removed who supported in even a minor way what was referred to as "bourgeois liberalization." At least four million people were investigated with thousands of officials deployed across the country to assess the political views of government workers. In addition to reaffirming communist ideology, this widespread crackdown instilled a sense of fear that to this day continues to dominate China. The brief period of relative press freedom also came to an end. This extended to foreign journalists who were expelled because they covered the demonstrations. Some were prevented from reentering the country.

With new leadership in place, Deng Xiaoping stepped aside and eventually retired in 1992. For a while he remained active in his program to promote the economic progress supposedly beneficial to the ordinary citizens of China - the same people who had just been murdered in the streets of Beijing. These events would have an enduring impact on China's communist party that never recovered from the episode. It was discredited as the group capable of safeguarding the revolution and its objectives. The old, ideological fervor, that inspired the early followers of Mao Zedong, was gone forever. Obviously a large portion of party members favored a complete dissolution of the socialist system in favor of a democratic way of life. Although subjected to comprehensive re-education, the rank and file could never be trusted again. In the future a combination of economic incentives and fear would keep everyone in line. *After Tiananmen Square the party was reduced to a caretaker role that for the most part involves administering the government's vast bureaucracy. Henceforth the ultimate power source that dictates policy shifted largely to the army and its inflexible generals.* Without their willingness to crush the rebellion in the harshest way, the system would have failed completely. A few years later in the Soviet Union that's exactly what happened. In contrast, China's military demonstrated that it could always be counted on, even if that involves murdering large numbers of ordinary civilians. The ascent of the PLA to a position of unopposed authority was engineered by a small group of party zealots lead by Dong Xiaoping. It was eagerly embraced by Jiang Zemin, enhancing his role even further. Having a natural affinity for the harshest methods, he had truly come into his own. Soon that was demonstrated by his sponsored program of organ harvesting to dispose of troublesome pacifists. As a favor the program was given to the generals as a significant source of new funds for the military. It is apparent that Dong and Jiang were kindred spirits. In a time of crisis they found one another, and the consequences would be enormous for China as well as the world at large.

During Deng Xiaoping's reign, an influential group known as the "Elders" met regularly at his house to advise on policy. It was an example of the informal way he operated. The group was comprised of revolutionaries of unquestioned loyalty, who represented a repository of party wisdom Deng respected. With the loss of the party's dominant role, the "Elders" were disbanded and a new group consisting principally of top military officers took their place. At the same time the group moved underground so such a significant change would not be noticed by the global community. With this latest assemblage of "Elders" becoming the new power center, the wisdom relied on now is unequivocally military in character. Of importance, the members of the group share a common, ideological obsession with an emphasis on force to further the interests of the communist state. What is certain is that for a long time there would not be another uprising in China like Tiananmen Square – although at some point in the future...

To this day hardly anyone inside or outside the country realizes how completely the PLA currently dictates policy. This is important so foreigners continue to pour money into China along with technical know-how. *Unaware of the true situation, the international business community is currently in the paradoxical position of being informal "partners" with the obsessive generals of the PLA.*

The new, power arrangement engineered by Deng

Xiaoping went smoothly under Jiang Zemin and later Hu Jintao. Previously Hu distinguished himself by crushing resistance in Tibet, making clear that he had the right instincts for the top job. During all this time Jiang Zemin never went away and even now remains a pivotal figure in the government's hidden hierarchy. It is apparent that Xi Jinping is more popular with the generals than Jiang, who had a very different person in mind for the top job.

Meanwhile Xi continues to amass even more power, far exceeding the authority in the hands of either of his predecessors. While all of this might seem an over-concentration at the top, the arrangement enables those really in control to have their dictates implemented in the most efficient way. With the recent internal reforms, every aspect of Chinese society is controlled now directly through Xi. Such an arrangement will be especially important during wartime. This explains why Xi is supposedly in charge of the nation's vast armed forces - a role for which he is not qualified. Such a responsibility seems self-defeating in the extreme. However, he doesn't need such experience because at all times he is implementing the wishes of the country's top military minds. The personal mythology constructed around Xi is an attempt to recover some of the lost, ideological purity that once was widespread in China. With Xi skillfully conveying the impression of the amiable despot, *world leaders are cultivating a relationship with an individual, who is essentially a hollow intermediary with little or no authority to make commitments.*

The apparent consolidation of all power in his hands also points to the fact the ambitious plan to wage World War III is moving forward rapidly. With the grip of militaristic fanatics continuing to tighten over the country's unfortunate citizenry, the innocuous sounding Social Credit Score is a key component of escalating, internal control that soon will be absolute. **In many respects this unfortunate situation is worse than the old Soviet Union. This is especially true regarding such ultimate decisions as when to initiate a war and what methods will be used. Tiananmen Square demonstrated vividly that killing large numbers of ordinary people will never be a concern for the generals of the PLA. They are the new, supposedly all-knowing "Elders," who currently control history's greatest Marxist- Leninist state. It is one in which human life has virtually no meaning and will be sacrificed as necessary in pursuit of the grandiose aspirations of a dominant China that transcends all.**

11

Throughout China a vast system of underground chambers of enormous size has been excavated deep in the bedrock. In this hidden realm millions of people can survive for long periods of time. Such areas are located beneath at least 35 major cities, including Beijing, Shanghai, Nanjing, Hangzhou, Jinan, etc. Most can accommodate a minimum of 300,000 people and some considerably more. All of the necessities for a normal existence are included. Over a half-century what has been created deep underground in China is a vast, concealed "state within a state." Scattered over a geographical area larger than the continental United States, this enormous, hidden realm has been designed to survive any assault, even one directly by nuclear weapons. There can be only one reason for creating something so bizarre and unworldly.

The sprawling area under Beijing exceeds 20 million square meters and is connected to 11 nearby districts and 7 counties through 20 communication routes. "Command" or control centers are located on four sides, and 170 entranceways are available to evacuate people from the city above. Under Shenyang City the area is considerably larger than the one million square meters already completed in 2002. Large, sub-surface areas have also been excavated in the remote countryside, especially in the mountainous central region often referred to as the "PLA's backyard." Little information is available about these remote locations except they can accommodate massive numbers of soldiers and equipment. The largest is the tunnel system in the far north facing the Russian border that has been under construction for at least 50 years. In total, the collective, underground areas assigned to the military probably can accommodate China's entire land army. Along the coasts of the South and East China Seas, there are hidden, submarine bases that the regime has gone to great lengths to conceal. Only a limited number of top officials know the exact location of all of these underground facilities on which so much time and effort has been expended.

Although the various components of this shadow realm are physically isolated, they able to monitor what is happening above. Some are interconnected, and all are able to communicate with one another. None can be observed from the outside, including from overhead satellites. As far as can be determined, every eventuality has been considered in their design and construction. The most noteworthy feature is the ability to survive a massive explosion in the immediate area above. Even if everything that exists on the surface is obliterated, the people and facilities secreted below will not be harmed.

For years outsiders have wondered about the numerous, unoccupied "ghost cities" located throughout China. In general, they have been attributed to an effort to provide work for the country's oversize labor force. While inflating GDP numbers, the ghost cities are also an important adjunct to the country's vast, underground realm. In the event some of the nation's traditional cities are destroyed during wartime, the unused residential buildings of the ghost cities will provide large amounts of up-to-date living space. In fact, there are sizeable, underground areas beneath many of the ghost cities that eventually can accommodate those who survive below.

Previously no society has undertaken such a bizarre, project, although a comparison is often made to China's "Great Wall" built many centuries ago. As a result some of China's military leaders refer to this recent creation as the country's "Underground Great Wall" because of its presumed ability to resist any onslaught. It is estimated that upwards of two million people have been involved in the construction work. Excavating deep in the earth is a hazardous undertaking and often involves blasting that can cause a significant loss of life. Most of the workers were probably convict laborers that are often used for government projects. Afterwards they are returned to prison, or if a matter is particularly sensitive, they are promptly executed so the available information is limited.

While this hidden "state within a state" is only one aspect of China's long-term preparations for war extending back decades, it indicates the character of the conflict that is being planned. Obviously China's leaders are willing to go to any length in order to achieve victory. This includes the possible use of nuclear weapons. Based on the project's overall size, a realistic estimate can be made of the number of people considered indispensable, who must survive to lead the country after hostilities end. It is approximately 20 million. Undoubtedly most belong to the upper echelons of the communist party or about one-quarter of total membership. While such a number is not inconsiderable, it is very small in comparison to the country's overall population. Mao Zedong and various, high-level officials emphasized repeatedly their lack of fear of nuclear weapons and the inevitable loss of life they cause. During World War III this number will far surpass anything previously witnessed in history's most destructive conflicts including World War II.

Currently an extensive sperm collection program in China is systematically acquiring samples from carefully screened donors. Only select individuals, who comply with the rigorous criteria, are allowed to participate. The requirements emphasize a favorable health background extending back generations and also certain desirable, physical characteristics. Apparently the regime views the potential loss of life during any future conflict as a convenient way of enhancing Chinese society. According to this flawed reasoning, the weakest and least useful will likely perish. With those regarded as "undesirable" disposed of, this will pave the way for a superior population. How often in the past has this insidious theme arisen in connection with various, totalitarian regimes. While the enforced culling of pacifists and dissidents has for years been used in China, an even more violent form will soon be directed by the leadership at the Han people themselves. It is ironic that *what is intended to bring about the long-awaited ascendancy of the Han could result in the direct opposite - perhaps their virtual destruction.*

Such a callous attitude toward human life also involves a willingness to use the regime's own soldiers in a profligate way - something demonstrated repeatedly during the Korean War. This mentality arises partly from the enormous manpower the communist state controls. In addition, it has deep, cultural roots harkening back to China's ancient history of absolute totalitarianism that emphasizes the primacy of an all-powerful government. Under the old Chinese Empire, Confucianism was replaced with a perverse form of legalism, in which the dictates of a remote emperor were inflexible and absolute. As a result some believe that China invented totalitarianism. The current rule of the communist party merely updates the process in which authoritarianism functions as an official "religion" with an all-knowing state worshipped instead of God. In this context the individual exists only to serve those in power and is valued accordingly.

Of late, in China there has been a renewed effort to destroy religious belief of every kind, especially Christianity. Long-established churches have been bulldozed or burned to the ground. In many locations the picture of Jesus Christ has been vandalized and replaced with the image of Xi Jinping. As the nation's new demi-god, he supposedly personifies the essence of the all-knowing state that can do no wrong. Recently the same bulldozers have been directed at mosques and other places of worship throughout the country.

All of this contrasts dramatically to the attitude that prevails in western nations, where the preservation of human life is a prime objective. Even the loss of a single soldier is mourned as a tragic event - a concept derived to a large extent from the Judeo-Christian religious tradition. These diametrically opposed views place China's opponents at a disadvantage during wartime and will have a significant impact on how the upcoming global conflict is fought. No doubt, China's strategists will attempt to inflict maximum casualties on any opponents in order to undermine their will even if it means squandering large numbers of their own soldiers and citizens.

While the construction of China's vast, underground world has attracted little attention, a recent, expansionist project with strategic implications has aroused considerable controversy. This is the colonization of the South China Sea accomplished by constructing a system of artificial islands on previously uninhabited reefs. Begun in 2013, this formidable undertaking involves dredging massive amounts of sand from the sea floor that are deposited on the reefs. On these reclaimed areas sophisticated, military installations have been installed.

One of the most important maritime passageways on

the globe, the South China Sea is vital to international shipping (30% of global crude oil trade). Specifically China claims historical ownership of the entire area demarcated by what is referred to as the "nine dash line" drawn on a map. This arbitrary designation encompasses Taiwan and everything else except the immediate coastal areas of nearby countries. Not surprising, there has been universal condemnation by the global community. In 2016, the issue was contested before the United Nations Permanent Court of Arbitration in the Hague that ruled China's claim a violation of international law. In response China has ignored the ruling along with the ongoing protests from the world community. Many recall a similar situation decades ago when China arbitrarily seized Tibet. Large portions of its territory were promptly annexed, and a brutal process of repression commenced that continues to this day. A similar process followed to the north in the Muslim East Turkestan Republic.

Of late China's military is acting with increasing belligerence toward any foreign vessels that enter the South China Sea. This includes American and British warships. Within the disputed area development has taken place on two, strategically located island chains - the Spratlys and Paracels. In the Spratlys hundreds of miles east of the Vietnamese coast, three of seven, former reefs have been developed - Fiery Cross, Mischief and Subi. Currently they contain anti-aircraft, radar and cruise missile installations as well as runways for military aircraft. The most important is Fiery Cross, where the rapidly developing harbor is large enough to accommodate China's biggest naval vessels. There are estimates that potentially this harbor will be larger than Pearl Harbor. A sophisticated sensor array indicates that Fiery Cross will serve as the principal communications hub for the entire region. In addition, the island's radar scrambling equipment has the ability to incapacitate the navigation system of most ships that enter the area.

The Paracels are located south of China's Hainan Island with its major, submarine base. Of the eight islands in the chain, six are currently being developed. Eventually there are plans for an "island city." Currently Woody Island has the largest military presence in the South China Sea (about 2000 troops) and is designated the administrative capital. The various facilities on Woody Island include a long runway, several airplane hangars and also extensive radar and batteries of anti-aircraft missiles. Some of China's most advanced aircraft are present on Woody Island and Fiery Cross including the J-20 stealth fighter. It is apparent that a key objective of the installation on Woody Island is protecting the Hainan underground naval base that can release large numbers of submarines into both the South and East China Seas. In this way the entire maritime region has been turned into what amounts to a vast, armed camp.

The strategically located Scarborough Shoal is also

under Chinese control. As yet only limited construction has occurred there, although it is only a matter of time before this area is developed as well. There are indications this process of creating artificial, maritime bases will continue in other areas as well. Recently a Chinese flag was planted on Sandy Cay only 12 nautical miles south of Thitu Island owned by the Philippines. Also a Chinese survey ship has been active over the "Benham Rise" *east* of Luzon. Potentially development of this sprawling reef could support a military facility of considerable size, impacting the entire western Pacific. As this expansionary process continues further to the east, it is possible that one day the Hawaiian Islands will be vulnerable to attack - something that only a few years ago was inconceivable.

All of this activity has taken the global community by surprise with China quickly achieving complete dominance over the South China Sea in only a couple of years. The belligerent attitude toward any outside presence suggests that an attempt is being made to seed the seafloor with electronic sensors. Combined with submarines, such a network would make it extremely difficult for any foreign vessels to survive there for long.

Another significant tactic to discourage intruders is the PAFMM (the thousands of vessels of the People's Armed Forces Maritime Militia). The world's largest, state-owned fishing fleet, it has previously been used for a variety of coercive activities. Short of engaging in actual combat, this mass of swarming vessels has been highly effective against opponents trying to cope with such a diffuse force. Prior episodes include confrontations over the Scarborough Reef in 2012; the Haiyang Shiyou oil rig; and in 2016 the Senkaku Islands. A parallel can be noted with China's ubiquitous, civilian maritime fleet that is constructed with a significant, military capability. It is believed that soon many commercial, maritime vessels will possess a high-powered, electronic rail gun capable of sinking a US warship at a considerable distance. In other words, when possible, every aspect of Chinese society is being weaponized so it can contribute to any future conflict.

The capabilities of the People's Liberation Army/ Navy (PLAN) continues to grow rapidly. The PLAN is one of the largest, naval forces in the world with *an emphasis placed on submarines*, both nuclear and diesel-electric. The number of these vessels is one of China's most closely guarded, military secrets. It likely exceeds the most expansive estimates. The future role of submarines cannot be overstated. The sophistication and size of both the East Sea Fleet and the South Sea Fleet continue to increase. These are the forces that would be used during any confrontation over Taiwan. Although China's strategists previously viewed its navy as primarily a coastal defense force, that has changed completely. Now the emphasis is on an offensive capability that can reach far beyond the country's immediate shores. The importance placed on naval power is indicated by the fact the commander of the

PLAN has been promoted to the most important, policy-making committee of the Central Military Commission. It is apparent the Chinese high command currently views the navy as serving a role equal to its army.

With the runways on some artificial islands able to accommodate the country's largest bombers, China's new-found offensive power can be projected far into the western Pacific and south into Oceania. As a result all of America's bases in the area, including strategic Guam, can be attacked directly. This rapidly expanding capability could one day prevent the US navy from being present in the entire region. The overriding question is whether America's largest, capital ships can be protected against a combined attack involving large numbers of submarines, airplanes and advanced missiles - perhaps those with a hypersonic capability. Currently US forces have only a limited defense against hypersonic missiles that can travel at six times the speed of sound and change direction during flight.

In addition, the character of the weapons being acquired makes clear the importance being placed by China's military leaders on the maritime environment. Since 2000 China has acquired more warships, including submarines and destroyers, than Japan, South Korea and India combined. From 2014-2018 a larger warship tonnage was added than the entire French navy. As a result Chinese naval forces have assumed a significant, global presence, its vessels often seen in such diverse locales as the Mediterranean and the Caribbean Sea near the Panama Canal. This capability is important to supporting China's newly acquired global network of ports and bases, especially those near vital, transportation chokepoints.

With America's role in the western Pacific being called into question, this could eventually leave Taiwan in a highly vulnerable position along with Japan and other allies. Not surprising, China is once again disputing Japan's ownership of the strategic Senkaku Islands in the East China Sea. Thus in a relatively brief time the balance of power in the entire Far Eastern theatre has been altered to a major extent - a process that can be expected to increase rapidly.

Through control of the South China Sea and other areas, the Chinese mainland can be shielded from an attack emanating from the nearby maritime environment. Because so many important cities are located on or near China's lengthy coastline, this will be essential to the country's survival during wartime. Its leaders are well aware of the capabilities of the US navy, especially its aircraft carriers. Obviously they are determined to neutralize this considerable force as much as possible. It is likely *that some of the most important battles of World War III will take place in or near the South China Sea. In fact, these battles could be decisive in the overall conflict.*

_____

Many knowledgeable observers have noted that China is acquiring advanced armaments at a pace faster than Hitler's

Germany prior to World War II. This is especially true of those with an advanced, high-tech capability. Similar to the Nazis, no effort is being made to conceal this significant development including the escalating expenditures for such weapons. Like all statistics coming from China, the published, military budget distorts the amount really involved. The latest, reported figure is about $200 billion, although the real number could be almost double that size.

Each year the Pentagon issues a detailed, annual report on the status of the Chinese military. Always the conclusion is the same - China is rapidly building an enormous, *offensive* capability aimed principally at the United States, its only credible opponent on the global stage. Of late China's land army is being restructured in order to project power more effectively over long distances. Previously it was used primarily as an internal force whose purpose was maintaining order within the national boundaries. A key aspect of this restructuring is a computer-based, operational command center that has the ability to manage highly complex, military operations over long distances - in other words the type that only occur during a major, expansionary war. Otherwise there is no reason to create such a group with its complicated structures and means of communication.

Rapid advances have also occurred in aerospace where America's longstanding superiority is disappearing rapidly. This is especially true regarding stealth technology. China's J-

20 stealth airplane with the highly advanced WS-15 engine is believed to equal the capabilities of the F-35. (In fact, the plane is based largely on F-35 design data stolen by Chinese spies.) The new Xian H-20 stealth bomber is basically a copy of the B-2 built by Northrop Grumman. The Chinese version has a payload in excess of 20 tons and can reach most of the western Pacific Ocean. These and other planes are fitted with the PL-15 extended air-to-air missile with scanned array radar, making them difficult to defend against. (This key weapon is also based on information stolen by Chinese spies.)

Recently China's intercontinental ballistic missile system was upgraded so it is able to strike any city in the United States. This includes long-range missiles launched directly from nuclear submarines. One of the most significant developments in China's sophisticated arsenal is weaponry used for advanced, electronic warfare. Of particular importance are those with a microwave or directed energy capability that can incapacitate the control systems of modern military equipment including planes and ships - in effect neutralizing them without firing a shot.

China is also developing an ability to incapacitate satellites (especially GPS) without which America's military cannot function effectively. The loss of only a few satellites would have a severe impact on US forces. Recently China began a program of supposedly managing space debris, which many believe is really a disguised effort to plant devices lethal to the satellites of other nations. In addition, a program to blind low-level visual satellites is moving rapidly to completion. This includes a system of observation posts scattered across China that will be connected to high-powered laser canons. The objective is to neutralize with energy bursts the sensors in visual satellites as they pass overhead. Such a beam travels at the speed of light and therefore cannot be observed. It is apparent that China has been working on this project for about two decades and has already mastered the technology involved. As far as can be determined, these satellites vital to America's survival do not have a viable defense against such an attack. In addition, a variety of means are being developed to neutralize the signals emitted by many satellites, some of which involve the 5G technology being rapidly installed around the globe. It is not an accident that China is attempting to dominate the new 5G system that has a much broader significance than current, mobile communications.

Also of note is China's development of hypersonic missiles; warheads that maneuver; and anti-ship rail guns, all of which are potentially lethal to the type of large vessels on which the supremacy of the US navy is based. Recently deployed on a limited basis is a rail gun with a range of 124 miles that fires a low-flying projectile traveling at 1.6 miles per second. Employing electromagnetic energy rather than explosive powder, such a projectile has the potential to travel upwards of 10 times faster than the Harpoon anti-ship missile currently in use by the United States Navy. In essence, such a device could be one of many game-changers on the high seas.

Ironically the weapon that could be the most significant during World War III is the one never mentioned - the neutron bomb. An extraordinarily lethal device, it is designed to kill people in the most efficient way rather than obliterating large amounts of territory. In essence, the neutron bomb is the perfect tool for mass colonization. In every respect it will facilitate China's upcoming invasion of the vast Asian mainland, quickly eliminating any opposing forces or unwanted inhabitants

In the late 1970s to early 1980s, the design of the neutron bomb (W-70 warhead) was stolen from the Los Alamos research lab by Chinese spies posing as scientists. Inexplicably they were able to access the lab's most valuable data. As a result they acquired 50 years of nuclear research by American and British scientists - the crown jewels of theoretical physics. This extraordinary episode established a pattern of lax standards that in many areas continues to this day.

Over the years China has been able to steal vital, American technology almost at will. *Essentially during this lengthy period the United States has functioned as the research and development lab for the PLA.* The cost to the Chinese government has been minimal. An open society like America is designed to encourage the free exchange of ideas, which opens the door to subversion on a grand scale. Tens of thousands of

Chinese students flood the research facilities of America's top universities, where they acquire the most up-to-date, scientific information. Many have been sent abroad solely for this purpose. In addition, corporate America continues to maintain high-tech facilities in China while many scientists move there in order to work in Chinese research institutes. Some have even been hired to contribute their knowledge to China's weapons programs. While this bizarre situation makes little sense, most people in the US don't believe that China harbors any hostile intentions. Unfortunately they are in for a big surprise, especially those scientists and businessmen living in China when World War III begins. It is not likely they will return. In addition, the enormous investment made by corporate America in China will be lost completely. Thus the pursuit of the great China market of unlimited profits will end in what amounts to a costly loss of enormous proportions.

Meanwhile history's most enduring Ponzi scheme continues to perpetuate itself through the oversize trade deficit, endless, fictional debt, and even more borrowing from outsiders who will never be repaid. **Thus in the name of globalization the free world's economic system supports a corrupt, authoritarian regime that has evolved into history's greatest threat to democracy and human existence itself. And so emerges the most troubling question of all - has the United States and its allies already lost World War III, having foolishly financed and abetted their own demise?**

12

With the balance of global, military power shifting toward China, the world community faces the prospect of history's first, truly high-tech war. Because of the weaponry involved, World War III will eclipse anything that has occurred before. Once again humanity is the prisoner of grandiose designs rooted in the quest for unlimited power that over the centuries have caused so much strife. At this point the existential crisis that lies ahead can no longer be avoided. Events have progressed too far. Through the grand deception perpetrated on the world community for decades, communist China (an ethnic, military state) has acquired the ability to realize historical ambitions that have long possessed its obsessive leaders.

Now military events on the global stage will be determined largely by which side has prepared more effectively - in other words dictate the way the conflict will proceed. Already China's strategists have put in place the key components of a swift, early victory. As a result the democracies of the West are currently proceeding at a significant disadvantage that will not be easily overcome.

More than 2000 years ago Sun Tzu formulated the concept of "*strategic siege*" that in recent years China's leaders have implemented so skillfully. Their attention to detail has been extraordinary. Throughout this protracted period they have demonstrated a dedication to long-term planning while never losing sight of the hidden goals being pursued. As a result the international community has been lured into what amounts to an enormous trap

While presenting itself as an aspiring participant in the global order, China has cleverly perverted the system to its advantage in every possible way. This includes signing and breaking important agreements; employing relentless espionage to steal advanced technology; and betraying every reasonable standard of forthright dealing. Through unfair trade practices, entire industries were taken over while competing enterprises were forced out of business. During this period of so-called "peaceful engagement," the communists were never interested in true cooperation with the outside world or improving the lives of their citizens. Always the central objective has been the expropriation of the wealth and technology of others in order to build a massive industrial base along with a powerful military. Perhaps the biggest deception of all is the ability of those who currently dictate policy in China to conceal both their identity and true objectives.

This mastery of the art of "strategic siege" is illustrated vividly in the much-praised Belt and Road project - a prime example of the way China manipulates other nations to their detriment. On the surface what is often called the "New Silk Road" appears to be a forward-looking example of international cooperation at its best. In reality, its primary purpose is strategic and especially military. In this way China has acquired a network of overseas bases reaching into every corner of the globe along with a vast, supply system that will be essential during wartime. At the same time the participating nations are subsidizing almost the entire cost. Through excessive loans many will eventually lose control of the facilities built on their territory and perhaps a significant portion of their vital sovereignty. In addition, the facilities are managed by Chinese personnel, some of whom are disguised members of the military.

This relentless process of silent aggression has been aided by the ongoing inability of the global community to grasp China's true intentions. Because so many are impressed by the country's economic progress, little thought is given to the real objectives being served. Neither the flagrant seizure of the South China Sea or the recent, mass internment of the Muslim Uyghurs (a rapidly developing genocide) has changed the situation. In addition, for decades the ongoing, highly profitable program of harvesting the organs of the country's pacifists has been largely ignored. All of this and more illustrates the truth about the inhumane regime that governs China. Glossing over such troubling facts has only made the situation even worse. With the country's military rapidly gaining so much strength, a fatal line has been crossed. A dictatorial state such as communist China acquires so much offensive power for only one reason. Eventually that power is always used to the detriment of other nations. In this case the ultimate target is the United States, the main obstacle to

China's ascendancy.

Like all modern tyrants Mao Zedong, founder of the Chinese communist state, had a far-reaching vision for his people that supposedly will enable them to achieve their rightful place in the grand order of nations. In this way the special character of the Han will be vindicated and age-old grudges finally addressed. Many in China believe their ancient culture is the most significant on the planet with far too many of its achievements appropriated by others. Since Mao passed from the scene, his successors have continued faithfully to implement his grandiose plans. Their commitment has never wavered, at times assuming a messianic character. The current situation would not be possible without the unique, Chinese character. This includes a remarkable capacity for discipline and hard work, especially as a group.

Now the climactic phase of the historical process initiated by Chairman Mao approaches rapidly. At its essence his vision emphasized territorial conquest on a grand scale. Previous installments include the seizure of Tibet and the Muslim East Turkestan Republic. These forced acquisitions effectively doubled China's overall size. The valuable, maritime realm of the South China Sea followed recently. All of this naked aggression has been accomplished with minimal interference from the global community, once again conveying a dubious message to the regime in Beijing.

The final component of Mao's far-reaching scheme

remains to be implemented - acquisition of the vast territory east of the Ural Mountains, a largely unoccupied area rich with valuable resources and arable farmland. From the start this great prize was always the focus of Mao's grandiose thinking. It is the one that finally will make possible China's ascendancy to the pre-ordained role to which Xi Jinping often refers. Supposedly most of the territory in Russian hands really belongs to China, having been stolen over the centuries when the country was weak. As a result the Chinese military will merely reclaim what was taken unfairly.

The preparations to seize this vast area commenced during Mao's tenure and recently moved toward completion with the acquisition of so much advanced, military hardware. Few except in the realm of science fiction imagined that such sophisticated weapons are possible. Based on ongoing, procurement efforts and other actions, key aspects of China's military strategy are already apparent. Particular emphasis will be placed on electronics, especially countermeasures that undermine communications along with command and control systems. The objective is to neutralize superior firepower while avoiding direct confrontations.

In warfare the unexpected usually prevails. As a result it is always difficult to predict exact scenarios. With so many imponderables rooted in the use of high-tech equipment, this dilemma is particularly relevant to the current situation. Therefore it is unavoidable the predictions that follow involve considerable speculation.

The long-term strategy of "strategic siege" is closely allied to *asymmetric or unconventional warfare*. Essentially the same underlying mentality is involved. Since the end of World War II conflicts among nations have to an increasing extent involved asymmetric strategies. This includes Vietnam, Iraq, Afghanistan and others. The emphasis is on surprise and the unexpected, in this way wearing down and ultimately defeating the opposing side. During World War III China's tactics will embody unconventional warfare in an elaborate form, especially involving advanced, high-tech equipment.

Another key premise expressed in "The Art of War" is that long-lasting conflicts are always ruinous. This is especially relevant for China with its huge population that in peacetime can barely be fed properly. In addition, there is the related problem of supplying its massive military with essential materials on an ongoing basis. This intractable situation represents the Achilles heel of the country's military planning. In effect, size is a liability as well as an advantage. As a result *China has formulated an ingenious plan to achieve a rapid and complete victory. There is a significant possibility it will succeed.* Also for years large amounts of essential commodities such as metals and petroleum have been stockpiled in underground sites all over the country. Some are even located under rivers. This ongoing effort has been a key factor supporting the artificially high, global price for many commodities.

Thus the added significance of the Belt and Road project with its extensive supply network becomes apparent. Important in this regard is the base on the east coast of Kenya that was acquired recently through a debt default. This valuable port leads directly into the heart of Africa, where China has established a claim on a large portion of the continent's natural resources. The coastal bases in Djibouti and Pakistan are also significant in this regard, protecting the movement of these supplies along with crude oil from China's close ally, Iran. In the Middle East, Iran is China's proxy that receives ongoing, covert support. This weakens America's presence in the area and also complicates the problem of maintaining control over the vital Strait of Hormuz.

After World War III begins, China's forces will need to dominate both the Indian Ocean and South China Sea. Inevitably this will lead to a confrontation with America's blue water navy and its aircraft. China's recently acquired base on the island nation of Sri Lanka at heart of the Indian Ocean will quickly manifest its significance. As a counter the US has its long-established base on Diego Garcia almost a thousand miles to the south. It is one of two, American bases with extensive air installations that will play an indispensable role in the upcoming war. The other is Guam with its proximity to the South China Sea. With control of the Indian Ocean in dispute, India's navy will become involved, although at this point its capabilities are difficult to assess. It is worthy of note that recently the US and India conducted joint, military exercises near Diego Garcia.

While the experience acquired during the sea battles of World War II is relevant, China will challenge America's navy in a very different way. Instead of surface battles on a grand scale, emphasis will be placed on submarines, electronic counter-measures and missiles that can be fired from hundreds of miles away. At all times the objective will be to avoid a direct confrontation with America's superior forces. This is especially true regarding its aircraft carrier fleet, the destruction of which will be a prime objective of Chinese strategy. As noted, a key question is whether such vessels can be protected so they are able to play a decisive role similar to what occurred during World War II. It is possible that some of America's capital ships will be lost - an adverse development devastating to morale.

Of late, large amounts of sensitive data regarding US naval strategy have been stolen from a variety of sources by Chinese hackers. There has even been an effort to penetrate the facilities at 24 prominent universities where important naval research is being conducted. This focus on stealing proprietary, naval information makes clear China's concern about this pivotal area. Obviously its strategists are aware of the limitations of their seaborne forces and are doing everything possible to address this problem as quickly as possible. None of this will matter, however, if *China achieves an early victory*. *At present they already have in place the necessary components to achieve such a result – and rapidly so. This is possible because of their extraordinary planning that extends back over several decades.*

Since the underlying cause of World War III is a quest for large amounts of physical territory, it will primarily be a conflict between Russia and China - one the Russians cannot win on their own. The disparity in the resources of the two countries, especially manpower, is enormous. Also the tactical problems for Russia are insurmountable. It is impossible for them to defend such a vast landmass, especially that portion adjacent to China. The logistics of moving and supplying ground forces over such long distances exceeds their grasp. In every way China will have the advantage. Also Russia's leaders have made an enormous mistake moving so close to China. To say that Russia's leadership under Putin has been "played" is an understatement. They have allowed themselves to be manipulated in every way because of an obsession with the West and the desire to overcome an enduring sense of inferiority. Once again in a major conflict longstanding, historical factors lurking beneath the surface have come into play. Now they have been inherited by the cadre of former KGB operatives, oligarchs and criminals who currently govern Russia.

Thus a pointless confrontation with the West is ongoing that accomplishes nothing, discourages valuable cooperation, and in every way harms Russia's vital interests. The relationship with China has been viewed as a counterweight to Europe and America, neither of which harbor any hostile intentions. While meaningless provocations emanate constantly from Russia, the real enemy goes unrecognized. In addition, Russia has foolishly sold some of its most valuable, military hardware to the Chinese. This includes their latest, 5th generation fighter, the Su57. Apparently the assumption was made that China already has its own advanced version. This is a major error of judgment. Rushed into production, the Chinese plane is incomplete and has significant flaws that can now be corrected with the help of the Russians.

Also there have been joint, military exercises, providing the Chinese with a detailed insight into the way Russian forces conduct themselves. The two countries share the same GPS satellite system, the design of which has been controlled to a significant extent by China. One day the Russians will discover how completely they have misjudged the situation. By then it will be too late. Almost a century ago the Russian leadership under Stalin made a similar, near-fatal mistake with Nazi Germany.

Many in the global community have wondered about the sudden internment of millions of Uyghurs in western Xinjiang. A key reason is the role Xinjiang will play in the approaching ground war. The presence of a large, hostile population in such a sensitive location is a complicating factor China's military is determined to minimize. The precise movement of Chinese troops in Xinjiang and elsewhere will be difficult to follow because of the new, anti-satellite system being installed across China. By 2020 the requisite laser canons should be fully operational. The loss of detailed, visual information will greatly complicate the problem of analyzing the progress of China's land offensive. This elaborate, laser system that targets visual satellites is another unmistakable indication of what China strategists are planning. Such a capability requiring years of expensive research has no other purpose except as a tool of advanced warfare. This is true of all of China's military preparations over so many years that include the acquisition of such a wide variety of advanced, *offensive* weaponry.

In order to take control of the vast Asian landmass, the Chinese face a number of significant problems, all of which they are able to cope with. Only a limited effort will be needed to subjugate the Far Eastern area immediately accessible from their northern border. This will immediately cut off Russian access to the Pacific Ocean. Over the years large numbers of Chinese nationals have crossed into Siberia. Undoubtedly spies and saboteurs are among them, which will facilitate this component of the campaign.

This initial step represents only a small part of China's overall plan, which is focused on subjugating Russia completely through massive force delivered in one, overwhelming blow. This is classic Sun Tzu theory. A key element will be paralyzing Russia's internal communications – in this way isolating various areas of the country from one another. As a result any coordinated effort to resist the invasion will be difficult, if not impossible. This will coincide with an effort to shut down global communications for at least a limited time – a capability that probably the Chinese already possess. Thus from the start the entire global community will be involved in the conflict.

After this initial step is complete, very large numbers of troops will be transported to pivotal locations on or adjoining Russian territory. These include the central, Asian republics; countries in the southwest accessible to China's close ally Iran; and even in the west not far from the Polish border. China has a heavy, transport bomber fleet numbering in the thousands - each plane able to carry at least 200 tons of equipment and personnel. In this way Chinese forces will be able to apply massive pressure simultaneously from a number of different directions. With internal communications compromised, such a widespread attack will quickly overwhelm the Russian military. *"Swarming" (the use of very large numbers of equipment and troops) will be a key component of Chinese strategy on both land and sea.* In the latter realm emphasis will be placed on massive squadrons of expendable submarines that will greatly complicate the problem of defending America's carrier groups.

The question arises as to when – not if – nuclear weapons will become involved. This is especially true of those designed for the battlefield. It is possible that a key component of China's massive, surprise attack will be the use of neutron bombs against at least some of Russia's cities. Delivered by missiles the effectiveness of this insidious weapon will quickly manifest itself. *In essence, what is involved here is an elaborate plan designed to eliminate Russia as a viable, sovereign nation.* If the Russian military survives such an attack, one defense would be to retaliate with nuclear weapons. Thus humanity will head down a disastrous path always to be avoided.

Potentially Russia could also attempt a counter-offensive, focusing the land war on the central Asian republics. The terrain offers a number of advantages. This includes the mountains along the eastern boundaries of both Tajikistan and Kyrgyzstan. This barrier will block China's infantry and armor and drive them to the north onto the eastern Kazakhstan plain, where they will be vulnerable to attack by air. In this way the Russians would be able to penetrate into western Xinjiang, putting China on the defensive. If the war does not end quickly, China will be fighting simultaneously on two, key fronts – central Asia and the South and East China Seas. These will become true, military cauldrons.

It is unlikely that nuclear weapons will be exchanged on a large scale between the US and China. To initiate such a process in an overt manner would be suicidal for the Chinese and lead inevitably to total defeat. Even with their enormous system of underground cities and military bases, they cannot survive two opponents employing such weapons. For the most part the conflict between the US and China will remain conventional and be focused on the high seas and in the air. Nonetheless there is a significant possibility that at some point missiles with nuclear warheads could be directed against American forces (mainly naval). This would occur if they gain a dominant position in the hornet's nest of the South China Sea. It will be essential that the US achieve superiority in this pivotal area. Ironically the artificial islands recently constructed by China could play a significant role in this regard. (It is worthy of note that recently US forces in the Pacific have been practicing amphibious attacks on small islands.)

If nuclear weapons are employed against American forces, they will emanate from North Korea - China's fully controlled proxy and convenient tool. It is the reason that North Korea has been able to acquire an advanced military capability. The underlying objective is that as necessary North Korea will do China's dirty work with its missiles. Potentially this could include directing them at the continental United States. As a result North Korea would be the object of any retaliation. In essence, the people of that abused country would become another of the many groups considered fully expendable. This even includes China's own citizens because ultimately there is only the all-powerful, Marxist-Leninist state and its obsessive goals that take precedence over everything and everyone.

DESCENT INTO DARKNESS

13

The internet designed as an enhanced means of exchanging information electronically has proven to be an enormous benefit to humanity. Unfortunately the internet can also be employed to perpetrate criminality, especially on a large scale. Soon it will facilitate history's greatest crime - World War III. Over the years the computer hackers of the PLA have tampered successfully with all of the internet's basic structures. While other nations are also involved in this perverse activity, China is by far the principal culprit. In this way its cyber spies have become familiar with the system's weaknesses, adjusting their invasive strategies as defenses are upgraded. In essence, the global community has created a sophisticated communications network that will soon be used as a highly effective tool of modern warfare. The importance of cyber space in the coming global conflict cannot be overstated. This is especially true <u>during the earliest stage when to a large extent World War III will be won or lost.</u>

A key target of these ongoing cyber attacks has been the world's infrastructure, especially America's electric grid. Grid function is based on control systems (Supervisory Control and Data Acquisition) that monitor and control physical infrastructure. This is executed by specialized computers referred to as programmable logic controllers that typically are the focus of attacks. In 2017, there were an estimated 20 instances where such systems were penetrated to a significant degree. Recently 60 utilities were targeted with the control systems of eight actually reached. In a number of cases blackouts could have occurred. During a successful cyber attack, malware can be planted for future use. This is especially true with programmable controllers that are designed to function automatically. It is reasonable to assume that such malware is currently present in at least some areas of America's electric grid. A major loss of electric power for even a brief period would be devastating for any advanced nation. All vital systems connected to the grid would be affected including the internet itself - the primary communication medium of global society. Thus it can be anticipated that *for a substantial period during World War III a significant portion of global society will literally go dar*k with the average person unable to lead a normal life. In fact, for a while few will understand what is happening to them. It could take weeks or even months to recover even a semblance of normalcy. By that time many will have perished while China's forces gain a major, tactical advantage – perhaps total victory.

It is not generally known that the air traffic control system can be accessed (indirectly) through the internet. In recent years a completely new system (NextGen.) has been installed that will be completed by 2020. As a result the traditional, land-based system relying on radar is being replaced by one employing satellites and radio communications that emanate from airplanes - ADS-B signals. The ATC system itself is not accessible directly from the internet but rather through behind the scene connectors that can be exploited in a variety of ways. Furthermore control systems are linked to business systems that open up additional vulnerabilities. The objective of modernizing the system is to make it more efficient by sharing larger amounts of information. As connectivity increases, a truly global ATC system is created. At the same time this increases overall vulnerability inviting intrusion by hackers. Consequently there is a very real question whether at times the ATC system can be impaired to a significant degree. Often thousands of planes are in flight over the continental United States. Even a brief loss of air traffic control would be disastrous.

The elaborate satellite system on which both America's military and the domestic economy depend is vulnerable in a variety of ways. This includes interfering with the signals emanating from the satellites - a task that is not difficult to accomplish. In other words it is not necessary to shoot down a satellite in order to impair performance. Recently a prominent analytical firm discovered that hackers had succeeded in taking operational control of a key satellite so it could be moved out of position. Also the potential role in this regard of the rapidly evolving 5G communications network cannot be minimized.

One of the most important developments with troubling implications is the ability of hackers to hijack the "internet of things" (IOT) - the vast array of devices (camcorders, home appliances, security systems, etc.) that are designed to be controlled remotely. On various occasions large numbers of these devices have been commandeered simultaneously (transformed into bots) in order to launch a coordinated attack through the internet. Furthermore, most of the electronic devices relied on by American citizens are produced in China and have chip-level, operating systems. It is likely that many contain undetectable malware subject to activation by a secret 1024 bit code. This includes at least some smart phones. Many US high-tech firms have discovered belatedly that a significant portion of their equipment has been altered for the purpose of espionage. A mundane example is power chords. As a result production of these chords was moved to Taiwan. *At this point everything electrical that has been produced in China must be considered suspect.* It is likely that when World War III begins, many of the devices considered indispensable by the global community will no longer function effectively except in a hostile way.

The broad capabilities of Chinese hackers to misuse the internet have been demonstrated repeatedly. Examples include the massive denial of service attack on the domain system and also the ongoing campaign to steal information from telecom and satellite companies. At times the most elaborate defenses have failed to thwart intrusions. In comparison, the average US household with a telephone and internet connection is literally a sitting duck. The full impact of what is possible in this regard is yet to be demonstrated. No doubt, in their bag of tricks China's vast army of determined hackers have some unpleasant surprises yet to be revealed. Unfortunately advanced technology ushers in the gloomiest possibilities. This is especially true because the gift that is modern, electronic communications can be perverted in so many ways. The only limitation is the whims of the perverse minds who engage in such activity that is no limitation at all.

It will not be possible for the United States to avoid being drawn into World War III. China's strategists cannot ignore America's global presence, especially its massive military. They must find a means to neutralize that power, at least for a significant period. The conspicuous success of 9/11 is obvious. As a result <u>World War III will likely commence with a stealth attack against US territory</u> - one that initially cannot be attributed to China or anyone else. This will precede the events on the Asian mainland and coincide with disrupting global communications. Once again such an attack will come by air, the negative impact far exceeding either Pearl Harbor or 9/11.

The likely target is America's east coast. It is not difficult to insert an anonymous airliner into the flow of traffic coming across the Atlantic in order to deliver a weapon of mass destruction. A "death plane" traveling at nearly the speed of sound low over the ocean would be very difficult to

267

stop, especially at night. There wouldn't be enough time.

China has made enormous advances in artificial intelligence that are being incorporated into its weapon systems. As a result such a plane would not require a human presence and could be programmed to self-destruct if necessary. The prospects for success will be increased considerably if the air traffic control system is compromised - even briefly.

The most likely target is Washington D.C., the location of the key, governmental structures that control American society. If such a bold move is successful, the United States would essentially be decapitated for a considerable period, greatly increasing the chances of China achieving a rapid, early victory. This is especially true if such an attack coincides with a campaign to paralyze overall, global communications. This includes commandeering the world's 4-5G telecommunications network along with the system of undersea cables. In addition, through its extensive system of overseas ports and bases with embedded forces (OBOR), China already has the ability to stifle surface transport, especially over the world's oceans. *Over a period of several years China's strategists have perfected these destructive capabilities. There is only one reason that they would have done so. Now the only question is when they will exploit them to the fullest and do so in a coordinated manner.*

Thus at the outset of World War III modern society as we know it could cease to function for a significant period. In this way the stage will be set for the massive hostilities on the

Asian mainland. These key, initial events will determine much of what follows. With such a substantial advantage already achieved, the Chinese military will be able to fight the war on highly favorable terms and possibly achieve a rapid victory. *This initial stage is the indispensable component of China's entire plan and must be executed successfully.* The global community must be taken by surprise. At this point that will not be difficult to accomplish. As noted, *all of the necessary components are already in place.* Once again this is classic Sun Tzu theory that emphasizes not going to war until the basis for a favorable result is already established.

While some in America are beginning to recognize the existential threat that is current-day China, few grasp the timeframe during which a major war will commence. The consensus is that several years or even a few decades are involved. In fact, time is running out rapidly as the options available to Beijing's strategists continue to disappear. The country's poisoned environment is having a debilitating effect on all aspects of Chinese society including everyone's health. Even industrial production goals in many regions are impacted to an increasing degree. Also the crisis in the food supply cannot be overstated. The economy burdened with limitless, fictional debt is teetering on collapse and eventually will experience the inevitable fate of all Ponzi schemes - even one as ingenious as this one. Meanwhile chronic corruption, financial waste and capital flight continue to undermine the system.

Soon it will be impossible to hide the truth from the rest of the world. China's astute leaders are aware of this fact and realize that they must make their move before the global community awakens to the threat. When that occurs, everyone will quickly abandon the hollow spectacle that has deceived them so effectively. It is amazing the Great China Scam has lasted so long. Meanwhile Beijing's strategists still have some breathing room. With their war machine dealing from a position of new-found strength, they know only too well it is essential that hostilities commence while the world community remains unprepared and largely in denial.

Before that changes, World War III will forever alter the global order and the lives of everyone on planet earth. After more than a half-century of careful preparation, the fanatical regime that is heir to the megalomania of Mao Zedong will not be deterred from their grandiose vision rooted in the distant past. At this time what cannot be determined is whether their remarkable scheme will achieve the success that eluded the other totalitarian states of the modern era. All of them failed in this grand quest that continues to lure humans at great risk to pursue the fateful dream of global domination.

Afterward

Almost 2000 years ago the ominous term "Armageddon" appeared for the first time and only once in the "Book of Revelations," the concluding chapter of the Judeo-Christian Bible. Over the centuries this cryptic reference has continued to haunt humanity, and during all that time scholars have been unable to agree about its intended meaning. What has never been in doubt is that this troubling admonition at the end of Scripture embodies a stark warning that a calamity of extraordinary proportions will one day befall the human race. In the late 20th century the world entered a period of ongoing crisis in which key events embody almost exactly what is described in "Revelations." Such precise parallels have never occurred before.

The "Book of Revelations" is one of the most extraordinary documents ever created. In the brief space of about a dozen pages, it explains some of the most profound truths of human existence. In fact, without this authoritative document there are some, important things humanity wouldn't know. This includes the purpose that underlies the historical process - an extraordinary tale that over the vast expanse of time is gradually playing itself out through a series of ages like the chapters of a great book. As a result each generation participates in events more significant than is realized.

What is particularly noteworthy about the current era

is the scope of incessant violence along with the perversion of "belief" itself, especially religious. Essentially the present era represents the dramatic conclusion of one of the most important ages in history. It commenced in the mid to late 19th century. Currently what is taking place around the globe is nothing less than the climactic resolution of the forces that shaped the modern world.

Because of the lack of formal narrative and unusual imagery, the message expressed in *Revelations* is difficult to understand. What is known for certain is that this final book of the Bible is the faithful record of the mystical visions of an unknown holy man named "John." At the time (late first century) he lived on the island of Patmos in the eastern Mediterranean and was a teacher highly regarded for his wisdom. In overall form *Revelations* is the pastoral letter of instruction he composed to the "seven" congregations of early Christians located in Asia Minor. In essence, those tiny, fledging groups were the beginning of what would become history's most widespread religion.

In this letter John explains what he experienced when allowed to visit the celestial realm, and departing from his physical body, was briefly "in the spirit." "A door was opened in heaven, [and then] "I John saw these things and heard them." He describes one of the extraordinary creatures that he encountered: "[the angel was] clothed with a cloud, and a rainbow was upon his head, and his face was as it were the sun."

What John learned at that time came directly out of the book held in the "right hand of him that sat on the throne" [and was] sealed with seven seals." - the great book that summarizes all others ever written.

Loosening the first, four seals reveals the legendary "Four Horsemen," who are given emphasis because warfare has played such a dominant role throughout recorded history. Always the horsemen ride together, inseparable in their violent mission. The first rides a ghostly, white horse and as the text states: "he that sat on him, had a bow; and a crown was given to him; and he went forth conquering and to conquer." The second is astride a red horse, and "power was given to him that sat thereon to take peace from the earth, and that they should kill one another." On a black horse rides famine, and finally the most ominous of all, the horseman astride the pale horse (devoid of all color) - "... *his name that sat on him was death, and Hell followed with him and power was given to him to kill with sword and with hunger and with death and with the beasts of the earth...*"

Thus the dreaded, Four Horsemen introduce John's account of humanity's tragic journey that through the ages has been dominated by incessant war and cruelty, a process that one day will culminate in an event of extraordinary violence - the great and climactic battle of "Armageddon." *It is this catastrophic occurrence that will bring to completion the long and tyrannical reign of the Four Horsemen.* Because of the devastation that is described, many through the ages have concluded that John was describing the end of the world - the name Armageddon becoming synonymous in most people's minds with this interpretation. However, the text doesn't actually say that, an important point that unfortunately is overlooked. Instead based on the actual wording of the text, it is apparent that Armageddon is something quite different - a violent, temporal event that will alter the course of human history and usher in a new age unlike any that has occurred before.

Later in the text it is disclosed that one day a great nation will lead humanity to Armageddon, when evil will achieve a great triumph in the desolation of history's most destructive war. In the past there have been many tyrannical regimes that ultimately fell in ignominy. During the current era the most powerful of all have risen in perverse glory - the modern, totalitarian state that has tried repeatedly to dominate the world. Not surprising, these states are virulently atheistic while employing false "belief" to mislead the masses and further a violent agenda. At no time in history has the process of human belief been distorted to such a degree; atheism asserted on a widespread scale; and the concept of a benevolent deity undermined so aggressively. In fact, deceitful ideology as well as mass murder can be regarded as two of the defining characteristics of recent, world history. While humanity supposedly has reached the apex of civilization, the most barbaric acts continue to be perpetrated in the name of the common man. Arising out of this chaotic situation, the battle of Armageddon will be the greatest act of mass murder of all as well as the most vivid embodiment of evil in recorded history.

In *Revelations* many specifics are provided about this seminal event that will commence in the Middle East, specifically along "the great river Euphrates... *[so] the way of the kings of the East might be prepared.*" Thus what occurs in the Middle East will be only the prelude to a much larger conflict that occurs in the "east," which is Russia and China. In that regard John states that "the number of the army of the horsemen" (invaders) from the nation that initiates these events will be "200 thousand-thousand" or 200 million. This is far more than all the world's armies together. John "heard the number of them" (was actually told) so it was not a guess on his part. Therefore those participating on the side of the aggressor nation will also include large numbers of civilians along with military personnel. Only China, which is synonymous with the "east" and at the time comprised at least one-fourth of the world's population, could be the source of so many people. ("And power was given unto them [The Four Horsemen] over a fourth part of the earth...")

Based on John's account it can be concluded that this terrible confrontation will dwarf anything that has happened in the past. The various descriptions suggest the type of devastation that can only result from the use of nuclear weapons - the ultimate tool of warfare and the preoccupation with violence. Because these weapons were only developed recently, it was assumed that destruction on such a scale could only occur when the world came to an end. With the development of modern, atomic physics, human beings have been afforded access to the most potent forces at the heart of creation. Now this great gift will be misused in the worst possible way.

The focus of this monumental conflict is given an unusual name - a Greek transliteration of the Hebrew term "Har Megiddo." Essentially a unique, linguistic construction, it means literally the "mountain of Megiddo," In biblical times Megiddo was a minor town or administrative center beside the plain of Esdraelon in northern Israel. Currently its ruins sit atop a hill about 100 feet high and not a mountain. John wasn't widely traveled, although it is likely that he spent some time in Israel, which isn't far from Patmos. Therefore he would have been acquainted with Megiddo, which appeared similar to the unknown place seen in his vision.

The nearby plain of Esdraelon is a relatively small place (only about ten by twenty-five miles) and could never accommodate 200 million people, especially since most are soldiers with equipment. Furthermore because there would be an opposing army, far more than 200 million will be involved. Nonetheless, as the text states, the war will be focused at the place "called in the Hebrew tongue Armageddon." Since "Har

Megiddo" means literally the "mountain of Megiddo," the location in question must be considerably larger than the biblical site. Somewhere "in the east" (China) there is a mountain vaguely resembling ancient Megiddo that will be the focal point of this greatest of all wars. Why this unknown mountain location will play such a significant role in this climactic event is one of the greatest mysteries of all.

In *Revelations* the ruinous aftermath of Armageddon is compared to the downfall of the most opulent city of ancient times, mighty Babylon. According to the ancients, Babylon's grandeur exceeded all others. In his vision John saw a great, ruined city on the coast of Asia that lay tragically in ruins. What city he refers to is a matter of speculation, although there are only a few possibilities. And so John states prophetically: "and [at the time of Armageddon] the *cities of the nation fell*, and great Babylon came in remembrance...Babylon the great is fallen, is fallen, and has become the habitation of devils and the hole of every foul spirit.. and the kings of the earth.. will bewail her and lament for her...and the merchants of the earth shall weep and mourn over her, for no man buys their merchandise anymore. The merchandise of gold and silver and precious stones, and of pearls and fine linen, and purple, and silk, and scarlet...and anointments, frankincense, and wine ... and the *souls of men...*"

It was not until the early 20th century that additional

information became available that explains the term Armageddon in greater detail, <u>including when it will occur and why</u>.

On July 13, 1917 (time of the Russian Revolution), a lady described as "brighter than the sun, shedding rays of light clearer and stronger than a crystal goblet filled with the most sparkling water and pierced by the burning rays of the sun" appeared near Fatima, Portugal. The mysterious lady is believed to be Mary, the mother of Jesus Christ. At that time she made certain dire predictions regarding the future of the world that have become known as *"The Three Secrets."* To confirm the validity of what she stated, a miraculous event involving the sun occurred on October 13, 1917. It was witnessed by an estimated 100,000 people. This large assemblage included representatives of Portugal's most important news organizations, who verified in writing what took place in the sky. This unusual event cannot be explained by any recognized, scientific criteria.

The various accounts are consistent, and everyone who was there reported seeing the appearance of the sun change in highly unusual ways. Rain fell most of the day, and after the sky finally cleared, the sun could be seen rotating and changing color rapidly - some referring to the "sun's dance." A reporter from *O Seculo*, Portugal's most important newspaper, stated that "the sun trembled, made sudden, incredible movements outside all cosmic law: *the sun "danced* according to the typical expression of the people." In the Lisbon daily, *O Dia*, it was reported: "the silver sun, enveloped in the same gauzy, purple light, was seen to whirl and turn in the circle of broken clouds...*the light turned a beautiful blue, as if it had come through the stain-glass windows of a great cathedral*..." Outside the immediate area of Fátima, no such unusual changes in the sun's appearance were seen.

Of the Three Secrets that were disclosed, the most significant is the Second. In essence, it takes the form of Mary's *explicit statement regarding humanity's immediate future.* Specifically the Second Secret refers to the rise to power of the Bolsheviks and atheistic communism (Marxist-Leninist) in Russia, an event that irrevocably changed modern history. In that pivotal year the great totalitarian state of the current era first arose in all its perverse glory and implemented an agenda that emphasizes mass cruelty as well as a virulent hatred of religion. It was the official position of the communists emanating from Lenin that religion was the "opiate of the people" and an obstacle to progress. As a result religious belief had to be eliminated by whatever means was necessary. A dark night of persecution swept over a vast country that previously was one of the most religious on the globe. Church lands were confiscated, and the number of churches reduced from 30,000 to less than 500 located in remote, rural areas. 100,000 priests and bishops were executed in the cruelest ways. In essence, a religious establishment beloved by the people for centuries was quickly decimated. Other religious groups were also treated harshly including the Jews who have always been persecuted in Russia. Both extreme violence and an antipathy to religion are the essential characteristics of all modern, totalitarian states. The obvious reason is that belief in a benevolent God impedes the ability of the state to dominate its citizens so they can be used in whatever way is considered necessary.

In the Second Secret Mary states clearly that if Russia did not return to its spiritual roots, communism would spread elsewhere resulting in catastrophic events of a global nature. Already this has happened. Additional *"wars"* (plural) after the First World War were predicted, indicating that violence on a grand scale would not end with the Second World War. Furthermore, references are made to "persecutions of the church" - the term used generically. Thus the religious beliefs of many kinds would be undermined, an interpretation verified by recent events.

On March 8-12, 1917 (new style or Georgian calendar), the Russian Revolution commenced, the event that gave birth to the modern totalitarian state. The czar formally abdicated on March 15, and on April 16th Lenin returned from Europe to Petrograd, the center of the revolution. On July 1ˢᵗ 500,000 Bolshevik sympathizers demonstrated, and an unsuccessful coup attempted two weeks later. Finally on November 7, Petrograd was seized, and the next day the Winter Palace, a key symbol of the monarchy. These events effectively gave power to the Bolsheviks and are often referred to as the "October

Revolution" according to the old style or Julian calendar that was in effect in Russia at that time. These events, that would have such a far-reaching impact, *occurred in the same timeframe as the visitations at Fatima. The chronological parallels are almost exact. In essence, the one (Fatima) is a response to the other, warning humanity in vivid terms of what could lie ahead.*

Specifically, the first visitation (May 13) at Fatima occurred shortly after the turmoil in Petrograd began to escalate. The Three Secrets (the second of which specifically refers to the events in Russia) were conveyed on July 13 or only a couple of days after the first attempt at a coup. At that time the success of the revolution was already apparent. The miracle of the sun, that was intended to demonstrate the validity of the Three Secrets, occurred only a few weeks before the Bolsheviks finally gained power. Unfortunately the Russian nation did not return to its religious roots and instead communism ("her errors") spread elsewhere "causing wars and persecutions..." The Second World War followed - a "worst one [than the First World War]...during the pontificate of Pope Pius XI."

Because it is stated that there would be additional "wars," we can conclude that another, major conflict still lies in the future. It will involve unprecedented violence with "various nations being annihilated." This terminology is very important, especially that *"various nations" will be "ANNIHILATED."* This word is probably the most important in all of the Three Secrets. Thus certain nations will not merely be ruined. Annihilation" is something quite different. It is the strongest term that can be used. It means "reduced to nothing." Usually warfare only damages or incapacitates a defeated nation. Rarely is such a nation reduced to nothing. During the Second World War several nations were severely damaged. Even after incessant aerial bombing, substantial portions of the targeted cities remained. In only two locations did true annihilation occur - Hiroshima and Nagasaki after they were leveled by atomic bombs. Pictures of these tragic cities demonstrate annihilation in the true sense of the term along with the nothingness that is implied. The "annihilation" predicted in the Second Secret will engulf entire "nations" and not merely a few cities. Therefore it can be concluded that one day a war will occur that is monumental in scope and employ nuclear weapons (World War III) - one in which a number of nations over a significant geographical area will be reduced to nothing. Not surprising, the imagery regarding Armageddon in the *Book of Revelations* describes almost exactly the type of devastation caused by nuclear weapons.

Also John predicted that arising out of the events in Russia during 1917, the world will experience not only "wars" but also religious "persecutions" - the other tragic legacy stemming from the rise of modern totalitarianism. According to the symbolic prediction that is the Third Secret, the assault of nihilism against religion will be ongoing and may conclude with the belief in God being destroyed completely. This ominous possibility is left unresolved. In other words during the 21st century, it could be the tragic fate of humanity to experience both the physical devastation of World War III (Armageddon) as well as a ruin of even greater significance - the loss of spiritual values. Thus in the end atheistic Marxist would finally triumph along with the denial that there is a fundamental world order stemming from the Judeo-Christian Bible - in other words an eternal God.

The destruction of western civilization and its key ideals, including religion and constitutional democracy, has always been the objective of Marxist-Leninism. Such a profound tragedy would usher in an enduring dark age in the name of false equality. As stated in the Introduction to this book, what is currently at stake for global society is *everything.*"

Note: Without the *Book of Revelations* combined with the disclosures at "Fatima," it isn't possible to understand the full significance of the Biblical reference to "Armageddon." In that regard see the companion book, *The Coming of Armageddon - History's Longest Night.* This fictional account of World War III explains in detail the predictions in these two, authoritative, historical sources and how they supplement each other – in essence, "The Three Secrets" updating "Revelations" to the present.